MORE THAN MOUNTAINS

THE TODD HUSTON STORY

One Leg,
Fifty
Mountains,

An
Unconquerable
Faith

TODD HUSTON WITH KAY D. RIZZO

Pacific Press Publishing Association
Boise, Idaho
Oshawa, Ontario, Canada

Huston Resources, L.L.C
Tulsa, Oklahoma

Edited by Jerry D. Thomas/Kenneth R. Wade
Cover design by Ed Guthero
Cover photo by Dan Miller
Typeset in Bookman 11/13

ISBN 0-8163-1250-8

95 96 97 98 99 • 5 4 3 2 1

Dedication

To those of us who have had to struggle.

THANKS

To reach the top of my mountains, I was assisted by the efforts of many. I thank God for these people:

My family, who was always there, and a source of encouragement and laughter;
Lisa, who worked hard and kept the faith;
Whit, for being there and sticking it out;
Our sponsors—John Shanahan of Hooked on Phonics; Flex-foot; and the individuals who were willing to believe and support my dream;
Ron Gladden, for getting the word out;
And to everyone who prayed for us—it really works.

Contents

CHAPTER ONE

The Foot of Denali

"Man is not ready for adventure unless he is rid of fear. For fear confines him and limits his scope. He stays tethered by strings of doubt and indecision and has only a small and narrow world to explore" (William O. Douglas, Of Men and Mountains [New York: Harper and Brothers Publisher, 1950], x)

The silence outside seemed to deepen as we headed north out of Anchorage. Inside the taxi, our driver kept up a steady stream of comments as he pointed out the sights along the way. "You could see a lot more if it weren't for this fog," he said apologetically. "On a clear day, you can see the mountain by now."

The mountain. Even in this land crisscrossed by mountain ranges, there was no mistaking what he meant. In this part of the world, that tone was reserved for only one mountain.

Mount McKinley.

Sitting 135 miles north of Anchorage, Mount McKinley shoulders its way above the neighboring peaks of the Alaska Range to a majestic elevation of 20,320 feet. Two thousand and four hundred miles farther north than Everest—only three-and-a-half degrees south of the Arctic Circle, the mountain wears a perpetual shroud of snow and ice; its moods are capricious and unforgiving.

The McKinley Massif, a cluster of twenty-one peaks, all more than 10,000 feet in elevation, has the world's greatest rise above the timberline, with the snowline at 4,000 feet.

William A. Dickey, a Princeton graduate who struck gold in the Yukon, named Mount McKinley in 1896. The caribou hunters to the north and west call the mountain Denali. Native people to the east refer to it as Traleika. Both Indian names mean the "Great One"—an impressive and appropriate name. Climbers call it Denali out of respect.

As we drove in, the mist partly swallowed our destination— the small community of Talkeetna. I strained for a glimpse of the mountain, but it, too, hid behind the fog.

"I guess you'll be staying," our driver said with a soft laugh.

I looked at him, puzzled. "Of course we are."

He shrugged. "Last month I drove a group of would-be climbers up here. It was a beautiful, clear day. They took one look at the mountain and said 'No way!' They got right back in the car, and we drove back to Anchorage."

With those encouraging words, the driver deposited the four of us and our gear in front of Doug Keating's Bunkhouse, where we'd arranged to stay for the night.

Climbers scurried in and out of the establishment like ants deprived of direction. I studied the faces of the people. Some looked tired and worn, beat-up after completing their tour on the slopes; others appeared eager and impatient to begin their ascent. I don't know what my face said, but inside I had a feeling I might not make it off Denali alive. I did an apprehensive 360-degree look at the small town. *Is this the last vestige of civilization I'll live to see?*

Impenetrable storm clouds, brooding and ponderous, hovered over the area, blocking all glimpses of the Great One. *What am I doing here? I must be crazy! Does God really want me here? Or did I make up the whole thing in my mind to prove something to myself? Or to God?*

I stopped a man wearing the typical climbing garb and introduced myself. A moment of small talk led to questions about the climb. "Are all these people waiting to head up to the base camp?" I asked.

He smiled. "Not all of them. Some are heading back home."

"Do you think there'll be a problem getting a flight up to the glacier tomorrow?"

The climber shrugged. "Depends on the weather. The pilots need a break in the clouds. This mountain makes its own weather."

The interior of the bunkhouse was no more impressive than the exterior. In the middle of the noisy room, cluttered with backpacks, gear, food sacks, sleeping bags, trash, and climbers, sat my fellow climber, Adrian. From his perch in the midst of our gear, he was separating the supplies we'd need specifically for this climb from the stuff that we'd leave at the bunkhouse until we returned.

Adrian, our guide, was more than just another climber. He was the current high point record holder. He had climbed the highest point in each of the fifty states in just 101 days.

I stepped through the maze, following our lead climber, Mike, as he led the way to some empty bunks. I stashed my gear on the floor, then spread my sleeping bag out in the middle of it to try for a few hours sleep. I shook my head at the noisy, crowded room and at the light coming in from outside. Climbers stepped over me on their way in and out. *How will I ever be able to sleep in here?*

"Ready to eat?"

Whit was the fourth member of our group. I looked up into his grinning face and smiled. *Come on, Todd. It's been a long day. You're tired and yes, hungry. And you're overanxious, admit it. Things will look better in the morning.*

The four of us trudged across the street to McKinley Deli. I tried to downplay my anxiety in front of the others but to no avail—I was scared.

"So, what will you boys have?" A burly short-order cook, his beard thick and wild, turned the hot dogs and hamburgers on a grill while he waited to take our order. "We got the best burgers in town."

You mean the only burgers in town, don't you?

We ordered a couple of sandwiches and some pizza, then headed for one of the empty rough-hewn picnic tables. We'd barely seated ourselves when a couple of climbers dragged themselves through the heavy wooden doors. By the exhaustion in their sunburned faces and the painful way they moved, I could tell they'd just come down. Wanting to learn as much as I could about the climb, I angled over to where they sat and introduced myself.

"What's it like up there today?" I asked.

One of the men shook his head. "Bad storms and high winds. We were locked in at Denali Pass for three days."

"But you did summit?" I asked.

Again he shook his head.

You climbed all that distance and didn't make it to the top? I stared incredulously. *How disappointing!*

"Somehow, the summit loses its significance in the face of survival." He snorted and took a swig of hot apple cider. "I'm just happy to get down off that mountain alive! I am definitely ready to go home—alive!" Home, he explained, was New Hampshire.

Here I was, a relatively inexperienced climber, hearing how seasoned climbers feared for their lives. *How can I ever make the climb?*

He excused himself to place a phone call. "My wife's going to be so glad to hear that I'm on my way home."

His climbing buddy stared into his cup of hot coffee.

"Really bad, huh?" I asked.

"It's an experience I'll never forget." He glanced at me with a haunted expression in his eyes, as if measuring his words by my reactions. "At 19,000 feet, I chiseled a step in the mountain and saw a climber's glove under the ice. When I looked closer, I realized that the climber's hand was still in it."

A shiver of fear coursed the length of my spine. "A human hand?"

"By the style of the glove, I suspect I came across a climber lost on the mountain in the early seventies. Twenty years, locked in that ice." He shook his head. "I consider myself to be a seasoned climber, but right now, I feel overwhelmingly lucky to be down here, safe and alive."

Oh, dear God, I'm dead. I'm really dead! I stared down at the slice of hot pizza on the table before of me. *My last supper!*

I'd never been so scared in my life.
Not during or after the boating accident.
Not even before my leg amputation.
I'd have to be crazy to try to climb Denali!

CHAPTER TWO

Tragedy at Tenkiller

Lake Tenkiller, Oklahoma

"Help me! Stop! Help me!" I screamed, swallowing and choking on lake water. "Stop!" I gasped for air. Tangled in the towrope, I bobbed helplessly in the water as the boat drifted dangerously closer and closer to me. I tried to bring my legs up toward my chest, but a greater force pulled against me. *Doesn't anyone see what's happening?*

I glanced about wildly for help, but there was no one. Inside the boat, my family and friends were laughing and talking, unaware that the engine had slipped into reverse, and the boat was drifting backward. Sheer terror seized me. *I gotta get out of here!*

I ducked under the towrope and flailed frantically at the water, trying to swim perpendicular to the approaching craft. But the bulk of my heavy yellow life vest slowed me down, and the boat's propellers seemed to be sucking me in. I seemed to be swimming in slow motion. I struck at the water, expending my strength as one in a nightmare struggles against an irresistible force.

Behind me, I could hear a gurgling noise as the engine grew increasingly louder. I felt a bump, then my legs being sucked under the water. I squeezed my eyes shut and fought to escape the death grip holding me. I could feel the boat propellers crawling up my legs as the surging waters tossed my

11

body back and forth like a puppy chewing on a rag doll. The boat stopped. It was like a bad dream. I just knew I would wake up and find myself in my own bed, safe and sound.

I opened my eyes. Silvery specks burst across my vision as I gazed up at the sky. "Ahh!" I wailed, thrashing about in the ever widening circle of blood staining the deep green waters of the lake. "My legs! My legs! My legs!"

"Hold on, Todd. Hold on!" My father cut the engine, grabbed my life vest by the shoulder, and hoisted me from the water. Hot, searing pain flooded my body. Terrified, I thrashed about. Blood spurted out four to six feet in a pulsating fountain from the sliced femoral artery saturating the sides of the boat, my father, my friend Clay Bird, and everything else in range.

I'd never seen so much blood before in my life. To allow him better access to my pressure points, my father moved my legs. The flesh from my left thigh flapped about uselessly. Strings of raw muscle dangled from behind my right leg. The skin tissue draped in shreds, like jerky drying in the sun, exposing the bone and purple flesh.

As I thrashed about, I could feel hands, pressing me down. I could hear my father's voice. "Settle down, Todd. Try not to move. Clay, help me here."

Clay gaped at me, his eyes wide with fright. My father shouted at him. "Clay! Snap out of it. I need your help!"

Clay shook himself as if he'd been in a trance. Brook Baxter, another friend, gulped, then vomited over the side of the boat. When my friend Emily Shepherd saw what had happened, she grabbed my four-year-old brother, Stevie, covered his eyes, and carried him to the far end of the boat. My body contorted with pain as my dad and Clay lowered me to the bottom of the boat. Scott, my twelve-year-old brother, gaped at me, his mouth slack; his face, ghastly gray.

"Scott!" My father grabbed for the closest beach towel. "Get up there and drive!"

Scott shook his head in horror. "I-I-I can't! I don't know how!"

"You have to, son! I've got to stop the bleeding, or your brother will die!"

Die? I shook my head. *I'm not going to die.*

"Hold on, son; we're gonna get you to a doctor. Scott, get to it! Now!" Dad shouted out the directions for starting the boat as my brother obediently scrambled over the seats to the wheel.

Hey, no fair, I thought, *Scott's younger than me and he's getting to drive the boat.* My father's words drifted in and out of my hearing.

I squinted up at the late-afternoon sun. The specks of light pelted my eyes like snowflakes hitting a moving car's headlights. Dizzy from the pain and from the loss of so much blood, I writhed about on the floor of the boat. Somewhere in the distance I heard the engine of the boat cough, then sputter to life. I felt the vibrating rumble beneath me as we lurched forward then sped across the water toward shore.

"Why me?" I screamed as my father wrapped my legs with one towel after another only to have it, Clay, and himself immediately soaked with blood. "Why me?"

I could hear my father shouting at Clay to hold one of my pressure points as an ever-widening pool of blood encircled me. My years of Cub and Boy Scout training penetrated my curtain of pain. I remembered the manual instructing Scouts who found themselves in an emergency situation to remain calm, and I quieted. "All right, nobody panic!" I shouted.

I clenched my teeth together to keep them from chattering and bit my lower lip. *Remain calm. Remain calm.*

My father used beach towels to try and stop the bleeding, only to have them soaked with blood before he'd gotten them into place. I averted my eyes from my mangled left leg by looking at my right leg. Ignoring the split-open kneecap and lacerations, I tried to move my right foot. It wouldn't move. *So, why won't my foot move?* I had only one thought on my mind—my paralyzed foot. "It won't move. I can't get my foot to move!"

My father patted my shoulder. "It's OK, Todd. We're doing everything we can to get you help. Hang in there, son."

For a time, I concentrated on trying to move my foot, but it wouldn't move. This worried me. During the fifteen-minute ride to the boat dock, I lost track of time. Strange, disjointed thoughts popped in and out of my mind regarding school, football, my friends. Silver spangles continued to dance before my eyes. When the boat rammed the dock, shock waves of pain shot throughout my body. I grinned through pain-glazed eyes into my father's ragged face. "Does this mean I won't be able to play football this fall?" I asked.

Without answering my question, he leapt to his feet, picked me up in his arms, and shouted to the people on the dock, "Call an ambulance. My son's been injured. I can't stop the bleeding!"

I glanced down at the pool of blood I'd been sitting in, my own blood, and in a barely audible voice, cried, "Oh, God, help me."

A stranger pushed through the crowd of spectators. "I'm a doctor. Let me help you with him." He helped my father lift me from the boat onto the dock.

"Can I help? I'm a nurse." A woman didn't wait for a reply but rushed to the physician's side.

I didn't think about what the chances would have to be for both a physician and a nurse to be on the same dock at the remote lake at just the right time to save my life, because I never imagined that I was in danger of dying. I just knew I hurt badly and was terribly thirsty. My tongue felt swollen and dry.

"I-I'm thirsty," I moaned. "I need a drink of water."

The doctor shouted orders as he worked over my body, "Get him some ice to suck on." Someone stuck a couple of ice chips on my tongue. My friend Emily patted my shoulder. "Be brave, Todd."

I nodded as a suffocating blanket of pain smothered my awareness of everything but my pain and my thirst. I fought against the intense numbness that threatened to engulf me, to swallow up my consciousness. Then from somewhere beyond me, I heard the wail of an ambulance siren.

Oh, good. Maybe I can get some aspirin or something, I thought. But when the emergency vehicle careened to a stop at the edge of the wooden pier and the white jacketed paramedics burst from the vehicle, no one was listening to my requests for pain medication. They were too intent on getting me to the hospital as quickly as possible. As they were loading me onto the stretcher, I screamed in agony. Suddenly I felt someone take my hand. My father's distraught face loomed over me, his eyes filled with concern.

"Dad." I tried to smile, but I could only manage to wince. "What's going to happen to me?"

He shook his head and moved his lips, but I couldn't make out what he said.

"Don't move, son," the doctor warned as the white-coated paramedics loaded me into the ambulance. I craned my neck to locate my father's familiar face.

"It's OK, son. I'll be with you. Me and the doctor." My father patted my shoulder. I looked over my other shoulder at the physician, who was talking with one of the paramedics. I couldn't hear what they were saying. Never having seen the interior of an ambulance before, I glanced about at the emergency equipment surrounding me. Even in my pain, my fourteen-year-old-boy curiosity couldn't be quenched.

The ambulance peeled away from the dock, spewing a shower of gravel and dust in its wake. I asked for medicine, but no one could hear me over the blaring sirens and the roar of the engine. The emergency vehicle sped along the winding county road toward the small town of Tahlequah, some twenty minutes from the lake. It screeched to a stop outside the town hospital. My head flopped to one side as the attendants rolled the stretcher out and wheeled me through the automatic doors into the emergency room. *Now, maybe they'll give me something to take away the pain.*

Immediately, the doctor who had accompanied us from the lake shouted orders at the hospital personnel. In the flurry of nurses wrapping my legs in bandages and sticking my arm with a needle to begin an IV, I tried to be heard. "It hurts. Can I have something for pain?"

When no one responded to my request, I begged for water. I was so thirsty. A nurse heard my request. "We can't give you a drink, but maybe some ice will help." I smiled gratefully up at her as she placed chips of ice on my tongue.

"Mr. Huston, you were lucky that doctor was at the lake today." The physician on duty in the emergency room pulled my father to one side. I strained to hear what he had to say. "Without his emergency care . . . well, you were just lucky, sir."

"Thank God," my father whispered.

"But your son isn't out of the woods yet. Our little hospital here in Tahlequah isn't equipped to handle this kind of emergency. Todd needs attention far beyond our capabilities. Muskogee is the closest hospital to handle this kind of trauma case."

"Muskogee?"

Muskogee? My thoughts echoed my father's words.

"Your luck's still holding though, or maybe your son has Someone up there watching over him. It seems that the hospital's surgical team is standing by at the Muskogee hospital. They were preparing to do surgery on another patient when I called them about Todd. They're waiting."

I didn't hear anything further that the doctor said. The same two paramedics who'd carried me into the hospital lifted my stretcher and headed for the emergency room exit. The ceiling lights passed above my head in a blur. I felt lightheaded. A strange cold began building deep within my body, as if I were being frozen from the inside out. My teeth chattered. *How can I be cold? It's July, isn't it?*

Along with being cold, I wanted to sleep. *Maybe if I just close my eyes and sleep for a while, the pain will go away.* I'd still received no pain medication. *I'm too tired to fight,* I thought. I closed my eyes as they rolled my stretcher into the ambulance.

My father climbed into the vehicle behind me. He squeezed my shoulder reassuringly. "Hold on, son. Hold on. We're taking you to Muskogee. They're sending blood down from Tulsa for you. Everything's going to be all right; everything's going to . . ."

"I'm so cold," I mumbled, my eyes still closed tightly.

"What? What, Todd? What did you say?"

I repeated myself. "I'm c-cold." But I knew he couldn't hear me. I could barely speak above a whisper, I was so tired. He must have figured out what I was trying to tell him, probably from my shivering, for suddenly, I felt the weight of additional blankets. *That feels good,* I thought. *Now if only I can get warm.* As the ambulance sped west toward Muskogee, my thoughts tumbled around in my head like sneakers in a clothes dryer. *I hope this doesn't mess up my plans for football this fall. I hope I don't have to waste more than a few days of my summer vacation in the hospital. Summer? Warm? How can I be cold. It's July, isn't it?*

I licked my parched lips. *I'm so thirsty.* Another wave of pain interrupted my wandering thoughts. I squeezed my eyes shut. *It hurts too much to think. If only I could go to sleep.* I was feeling irritated with the paramedics who seemed to be constantly poking and prodding and shifting my body. *Why won't they let me sleep for a while, just a little while . . .*

Two hours after the accident, the vehicle screeched to a stop outside the Muskogee General Hospital. Seconds later, the ambulance's rear doors swung open, and a team of orderlies hauled the stretcher from the vehicle. I found myself surrounded with a horde of news reporters and photographers.

My father shouted, "No pictures! No pictures!" pushing and breaking the pathway for the paramedics into the emergency room. Once again, I screamed in pain as they transferred me onto an examination table, where I was twisted, turned, examined, and prodded. I alternately screamed and groaned from the intense pain each movement sent coursing through my body.

Somewhere between the ambulance and the examination room, I lost track of my father. Suddenly I realized that I was surrounded by polite, but anxious strangers, intent on their tasks.

Shifting me to the gurney, they wheeled me to radiology and lifted me onto a cold, hard metal table. When they lifted my legs to place the X-ray plates beneath them, I shrieked from the intense pain. "It hurts. It hurts too much! I can't take it any longer!"

"Soon, Todd," one of the nurses assured me. "The doctors will help you soon."

Soon . . . soon . . . I repeated over and over again in my mind as I tossed my head back and forth to relieve the pain. After what seemed like forever, they wheeled me into an elevator. I watched the lighted numbers on the wall of the elevator drop to the basement. The elevator stopped, and the doors slid open. Down a hallway to another set of doors. They wheeled me through the doors and into a green-tiled room. Clanging instruments and machines moved past me. I glanced around at all the knobs, gauges, and switches. The sanitary "hospital" smell seemed overwhelming. Strong hands lifted me onto the cold, hard operating table. The room swarmed with masked nurses and doctors scurrying about, performing a variety of tasks. I closed my eyes against the blinding light.

I could hear two male voices discussing whether or not to amputate someone's leg. *Must be talking about another patient,* I reasoned. A slight man with kind blue eyes stood behind my head, talking to me, telling me to count backward from one hundred. He placed a mask over my mouth and nose. At the last minute, I squinted up at a large wall clock— 7:00. *Three hours since . . .* My pain faded. I felt a sweet, dizzying relief; then I felt nothing at all.

I awoke in the middle of the night in the Intensive Care Unit. The tube up my nose, carrying oxygen to my lungs, burned like fire. I glanced at the IVs in my arm and winced. My mouth was so dry, I could barely talk. "Water . . ."

Disorientated, I called out for my mother. Instead of my mother, I heard a stranger's voice. "It's all right, Todd. Your mother's waiting just outside. I'll go get her."

Outside? Outside where?

"Where am I?"

"You're in the hospital. You had surgery, remember?"

I nodded absently. "I think so." Then suddenly the memory of the boating accident hit me. *My legs!*

With one arm strapped to a board for the intravenous needle, my free hand flew to my thighs. *They're both still there!* Relieved, I fell back against the pillow. *Everything's OK. I still have my legs!*

CHAPTER THREE

Hope and Disappointment

Talkeetna, Alaska

Sleep came slowly in the bunkhouse. Even over the chatter and bustle of the other climbers, I could hear the words of a man experienced on McKinley.

"The worst thing a climber can do is push himself beyond his endurance," the man cautioned. "Slow and easy is the key to success. And on this mountain, success means staying alive!"

Who am I kidding? I wondered. *Can a man with only one leg really survive a McKinley climb? How hard can I push myself without endangering the success of the expedition? Or without risking my life?*

But I'd been pushing myself for a long time. Since the days I had slept in the Intensive Care Unit at Muskogee Hospital.

In those first days after the accident, sleep became a close friend. Lying peacefully on the bed, I'd feel an occasional pull on my arm, or a light in my face. My narrow, windowless room was barely large enough for the bed. I thought they wanted me to rest, but every few hours the nurses would come to draw blood, take my vital signs, or change the IV. I decided that hospitals are no place to rest.

I vaguely remember my parents coming and going from Intensive Care over the next few days. The doctors who worked on my leg came by regularly. Snippets of conversations broke through the barrier the pain medications built around me.

"Lost three-fourths of his blood . . ."

"Forty stitches on his left leg."

"Not enough skin on his right leg to close the wound."

"We seriously considered amputating the right leg."

"One lucky guy!"

"God must have been with him!"

When I fully regained consciousness, my mother was sitting on a chair next to my bed. Her purse sat on the metal table beside my bed. A newspaper protruded from it. I grabbed the paper with my free hand. There, on the front page, was an article about me.

I laughed when I read that I was in "critical condition" at the Muskogee Hospital. "That's silly. I don't feel 'critical.' " I didn't realize how much of my sense of comfort was due to the pain medications and not to my own well-being.

"Son, you don't know how close we came to losing you," she scolded gently. "When they told me over the telephone what happened, I was sure . . ." Her voice broke. She dabbed at her eyes with a Kleenex tissue. ". . . you wouldn't make it to the hospital alive."

"Aw, Mom." I hated when my mom got all teary. "I'll be up and out of here in no time, you'll see."

She turned her face from me, momentarily, then patted my arm. "We just thank God that we still have you, son."

"Thank God?" I'd always said my prayers, but I hadn't really thought much about prayer itself. Alone in my room after visiting hours, I stared at the ceiling overhead, alternately counting the holes in the Celetex and crying, "Why me, God? Why me?"

After a week in ICU, they moved me to a regular room. I had my own room at home. Having a roommate who coughed and groaned in the night made sleeping almost impossible.

"Why me, God? Why did this have to happen to me?" When I wasn't pleading with God for answers, I was crying out to the nurses for pain medication. I felt I no longer had any control over my life or body. Everyone else decided my fate.

In spite of my discomfort, I enjoyed the attention I was getting. I received letters and cards from complete strangers telling me that they were praying for me. Church members came to visit. My friends came down from Tulsa in groups, bringing all kinds of gifts. I felt like a celebrity.

One of my buddies gave me a red felt hat with a small feather stuck in the band. I liked the strange little homburg and wore it whenever the hospital attendants moved me from my room.

Friends helped ease the pain. My teammate, Mike, came to visit whenever he could. He'd tell me the latest news about my other buddies, and we'd argue about which team would win the World Series. My friends DeAnn, a cheerleader, and Emily, who'd been on the boat the day of the accident, kept me up to date on who was dating whom and who'd broken up with whom. My friends and I talked about everything except football. Whenever I brought up the subject, they'd change it.

Football had been my life. As middle linebacker, I held the record for the most tackles for my team during seventh and eighth grade. I was eager to get back to the game, especially with the new school term approaching. Of course, first I needed to be able to get out of bed.

Ten days after the accident, my mother gave birth to my little sister at the Tulsa hospital. The week after her delivery seemed interminable to me. Finally, her doctor gave her permission to make the drive to Muskogee. A family friend, Dr. Miller, a dentist, filled in and came to visit whenever my parents couldn't. He'd sit with me for hours while I chewed the Trident gum he always brought.

A pseudomonas infection developed in my leg. It turned my bandages green and smelled like rotten eggs and vomit. Every other day the orderly wheeled me to the operating room, where the medical team would put me to sleep in order to change the bandages on my legs.

One day they attempted to change the bandages without first sedating me. As they lifted the first layer of gauze, a searing pain shot through my leg, far worse than what I'd endured immediately after the accident. I screamed so loud and so long, other staff members in the hospital came running to find out what was happening. From then on, the physicians made certain I was well sedated before beginning the necessary procedure.

After a few weeks in the hospital, I began to realize that maybe I wouldn't make the football team at school. What I didn't know was that the surgeons had told my parents that my right foot was paralyzed and due to my extreme injuries, I would probably never walk again.

The sultry temperatures of summer lingered into autumn, and the new school term began for my friends, but not for me.

Less than two months had passed since the accident, and I was still far from well. During the eight weeks I was hospitalized, I endured twenty-eight surgeries. I received continued shots of Demerol for the pain. The back of my right leg was but a thin layer of skin grafted from my stomach. There were twelve inches of stitches on my left leg as well. Both my stomach and my leg looked ugly and burned. And each day, they wheeled me to physical therapy, where I spent time in the whirlpool, a thoroughly painful experience.

My body shrank from lying in bed. I felt weak and ugly, despite the ever-present red hat I continued to wear on my head. As I wasted away in the hospital, I continued to question God, to pray for an answer as to why I should go through such pain.

To build up my arm muscles and to help me shift my body in the bed, I used a pull-up bar over my head. After each exertion, I would flop back against my pillow, fighting a bout of fresh tears, remembering how my friend Clay Bird and I used to flex our muscles to demonstrate our strength. I looked with disgust at my emaciated body. *And now this?*

I moved from the bed to a wheelchair, to crutches, to walking with the aid of a shoe with an ugly metal brace that kept my right foot from drooping. The day I left the hospital, I did so on crutches, wearing my red hat and the hated brace.

I loved the excitement of coming home in the back of Coach Smiley's station wagon to a party in my honor with banners, streamers, and balloons. But when that faded, it grew more painful each day to watch my brother and his friends head for school.

My parents arranged with the school district for me to be tutored by a home-bound teacher. In my fourteen-year-old mind, the year stretched out into what seemed to be an eternity. I remember the day the reality of my situation registered in my mind.

Tears of self-pity welled up inside of me as I sat on the hard wooden bleachers, watching the ninth-grade team scrimmage. *I should be out there playing!* I swallowed hard, gulping back my disappointment.

I had been the one whom other teams worried about. Now, I sat at the edge of the field, my muscles atrophied. *I'm not a threat to anyone—I'm nothing but a weak cripple.*

Somehow, regardless of my pain, I couldn't accept the seriousness of my injuries. The pain of not being on the field with my buddies stung. Not to be able to play the game at which I was so good hurt.

"Maybe next year," I muttered.

"Maybe so." My dad squeezed my shoulder to reassure me. My mom dabbed her eyes with her handkerchief.

At home, I chafed under the imposed limitations. When I complained to my mother about not returning to school, she reminded me, "Todd, don't complain. Just that you're alive is a miracle in itself. Think about it." She shook her head in wonder. "What were the chances that a physician and a nurse, separate of one another, would just happen to be on the dock when Dad brought you in off the lake? That's not chance; that's evidence of God's love for you, son. I thank God every day that the medical team was standing by in the Muskogee Hospital ready and available to perform the necessary surgery that saved your life!"

"I know, but . . ."

"No buts! When I got to the lake, the nurse who helped care for you as much as told me you wouldn't live to reach the hospital in Tahlequah. You have everything to be thankful for, son." She clicked her tongue in agitation. "Losing three-fourths of your blood like that. Your father says that during the ambulance ride to Muskogee the attendants feared they would lose you when you went into shock."

I turned my face to the wall. I felt trapped, isolated from everyone. Yet I knew she was right. I was grateful to be alive, as grateful as any fourteen-year-old boy could be watching from the sidelines as his buddies caught football passes and tackled quarterbacks.

"You know that the doctor told us after your surgery that you probably would never walk again. And there you were, eight weeks after the accident, walking out of the hospital like you did."

"I-I guess you're right. But it's not easy." I glanced back at my mother. Her eyes were filled with tears.

"If I could do anything, anything to take away the pain."

"I know, Mom." I sighed and stared up at my bedroom ceiling. "I know."

"We don't always understand how God is leading in our lives, but He is, you know." Her voice caught. "He is. God has a plan for our lives. We don't always know right away what that plan may be, but if we keep asking, He will show us. Remember, all things work for our good, for those who love the Lord."

Averting my eyes from hers, I flexed and unflexed the muscles in my jaw.

While my family attended church each week, I'd never thought much about how God wanted to work in my life. And for the life of me, I couldn't see how this tragedy could possibly be a part of His plan. For me, church was the place to meet my friends on the weekend. Sometimes a group of us would find a back room where we would play spin the bottle with the girls or other such adolescent games out of the eyesight of the adults. However, since the accident, everything in my life had changed.

My friends dropped by regularly to see me, and I appreciated that, but their visits didn't compensate for all I was missing. I was so lonely. I found the class work to be easy, and my grades were good. I returned to the classroom second semester and discovered that I was far behind my peers. I spent the rest of the year struggling to catch up scholastically, socially, and emotionally.

When my friends learned I would still not be able to participate in school sports, the captain of the girls' football team made me a proposition. "Todd, you know a lot about football." DeAnn approached me one afternoon after freshman math class. "Would you be the head coach for our powder puff team?"

"I don't know," I drawled. I wasn't sure I wanted to get involved with the girls' team. What would my buddies think—coaching the powder puff team?

"Aw, come on. You'd be good at it. You know so much about the game," she coaxed.

"I'll think about it," I promised. Over the next few days, the girls on the team coaxed and bribed me with donuts and soft drinks. Finally I agreed. Within a short time, I decided coaching the girls was more fun than playing the game with the guys.

The metal brace I wore to hold my dropped foot in place rubbed against my skin, producing sores on my leg. While I couldn't feel the sores due to nerve damage, the infections would affect the rest of my body. I missed a lot of school the rest of that year.

Being a typical teenager, I felt self-conscious about the way my leg looked. On the back of my right thigh, I could see the huge gap of missing tissue and the bulb of hamstring muscle through the red and inflamed skin. The tissue would go for a ways, then stop where the propellers ripped it out.

I tried to hide my physical scars from my friends. I seldom swam in public due to my atrophied leg and the ugly scars. I used humor to hide the mental scars. I would joke about all the well-fed fish in Lake Tenkiller.

I dated a number of girls. But always, when we'd break up, I'd accuse the girl unfairly, "You don't like me because of my leg!" I couldn't believe the breakups could be due to the usual reasons high-school couples dissolve relationships.

I learned how to turn my brace into an advantage. When I played neighborhood football, I'd take off the brace and use it as a slingshot to trip up a person running with the ball. Otherwise, I found my brace to be ugly and cumbersome, a constant source of pain and embarrassment.

My sophomore year of high school passed uneventfully until one day a friend named Ken stopped me in the hall at school. "Hey, Todd, did you know that Doug is making fun of you behind your back?"

"No, what's he saying?" I narrowed my eyes. I'd never really liked the guy anyway.

"He's calling you the crip with the harelip."

Finally, an excuse to let go of some anger. "Oh, he is, is he?"

Being a typical teenager, I felt insecure about my body. But the problem was exacerbated by the fact that I'd been born with a harelip and cleft pallet, for which I had had four surgeries before the age of three. I felt self-conscious about the disfigurement. And now, after the accident, I was even more sensitive.

"Yeah. Ya want me to deck him for you?" My friend looked too eager.

"Thanks, but I'd rather do it myself. Where is he?"

Ken gestured with a nod toward the gym lockers. "He went in there a few minutes ago."

"Thanks." I set off toward the lockers. As I rounded the corner in the boys' locker room, I spied my nemesis removing his gym clothes from his locker. Without warning, I came up behind him, grabbed him, spun him around, and crashed him against the bank of lockers. "What's this I hear about you going around and calling me 'the crip with the harelip'?"

"Hey, man, I-I-I . . ." he sputtered.

"Don't deny it." I tightened my hold on his collar and leaned forward, my face in his. "I would suggest you stop calling me names, right now. Do you understand?"

His head bobbed in rapid agreement. "Yes. OK, I'll stop. I promise," he said in a shaky voice.

"I mean it."

"Right, man. It's cool. No more names."

I jerked his collar for emphasis, then released him. He rubbed his neck and averted his eyes from mine. I walked away satisfied. To my knowledge, he kept his word.

My junior year, I went through several operations to get the skin grafts to take on the back of my leg. At one point, I was in a body cast for months with my arm surgically sewn to the back of my leg in order to keep a blood supply going from my arm to the skin on my leg. They attempted a nerve graft by trying to reconnect the missing nerve in my right leg in order to overcome the paralysis in my foot. It seemed like torture to me, but in the end, it didn't work. A pattern began to form— hope for recovery followed by disappointment.

As a result I missed more school the next term, and I lost so much weight and muscle that my spinal cord protruded. It got to where I couldn't sit in a chair comfortably, and I was rubbing sores on my backbone. Disgusted with what was happening to my formerly husky body, I decided I would work out by lifting weights.

I almost quit before I began when I couldn't lift more than forty pounds. But day after day, I continued, adding push-ups to my workout until after a year of hard work I won the arm, wrestling championship at school. What my legs couldn't do, I determined my upper body would do. I built up my muscles until I could bench-press 200 percent of my weight. These sports helped build back my self-esteem. Maybe I wasn't physically helpless after all.

It was near the end of my senior year when I noticed a black blister underneath my heel, a pressure sore. By the time I discovered it, the blister had become infected and had broken open. The skin around it had died; the infection had spread to the bone. I managed to graduate, though I guzzled large quantities of champagne to get me through the graduation exercises.

The infection in my foot worsened throughout the summer and into my freshman year of college. Blood dripped out of my foot wherever I walked. I was in and out of the hospital with osteomyelitis in the heel bone. The infection spread to the rest of my body, producing fevers so that I seldom knew if the day's temperatures were high or low. The fevers sapped my energy and dampened my enthusiasm. I didn't know from one day to the next if I'd be in classes or in bed.

My problem continued into my sophomore year of college. At nineteen, I was a member of a fraternity; I had no money problems and no worries, except for the inconvenient crimp my foot put in my daily life. Intellectually, I knew I had it made. Everything externally was good, at least as the world defined it. *Then why am I so unhappy?*

Niggling at the edges of my busy life were questions, questions about God and my relationship with Him. All the years I'd attended church with my parents, I'd never made it *my* religion. And now, for some unexplainable reason, I felt compelled to recommit myself to Christ. I started reading my Bible.

When I mentioned my desire to a couple of my friends whom I knew attended church regularly, they began studying the Bible with me.

The more I studied, the more I knew I needed to make a decision. But I couldn't. I liked my lifestyle. I liked partying with my friends. I liked being free to do whatever I wanted, not having to answer to anyone. *I don't want things to change,* I reasoned. *Besides, I've given up enough over the years. I'm just getting to where I'm free.*

I wrestled with my decision for more than a week. On the weekend, I went home and told my parents about my struggle.

My mother, who was studying for the ministry, cried, "I'm so glad you came home and told us. We've been praying for you."

"You'll make the right choice, son," my father assured me. "We know you will."

On the way back to campus, I couldn't get their words out of my mind. I cranked up the radio to full volume, hoping to drown out the voice of God tugging at my heart. But a calm, gentle voice kept persistently calling. I choked back tears that threatened to destroy my resolve.

Pounding my fist on the steering wheel, I cried, "No way, God! No way! I can't make that kind of commitment to You, Lord."

Sudden oncoming lights startled me. I swerved to avoid an accident. Slowing to a stop beside the road, I put the engine in neutral, leaned my head against the car's headrest, and closed my eyes. "There's no advantage, Lord, to following You! No fun! It will interfere with everything I enjoy, my dating, my partying, my goals, my dreams—everything!"

Except for the courting ritual of a couple of crickets, the silence of the night settled around me. I gazed out the window at the myriad of stars in the Oklahoma sky. I swiped at the tears coursing my face and swallowed hard. "Can't we just take this step by step, no big decisions, just a little at a time?"

No voice spoke to me out of the darkness; no reply came to ease my pain. After classes the next day, I took my Bible and walked to a park near the campus. Settling myself beneath a tree beside a quiet stream, I opened my Bible and started reading from the book of Psalms.

It's not that I ran across just the right text to tell me what to do. I already knew what I should do. Finally, I struggled to my feet and looked up through the branches and leaves into the sky. "Lord, I'm Yours."

CHAPTER FOUR

The Decision

Los Angeles, California

A co-worker stuck his head around my office door one afternoon. "Todd, we got this press release on something called the '50 Peaks Project' in the mail today." He handed me the advertisement describing a Chicago-based organization's intentions of climbing the highest peak in each state in the nation. Curious, I read the attached letter.

"The team will be comprised of three disabled persons, including a blind person, a senior citizen, and a leg amputee. We have filled the first two slots and are looking for a leg amputee to join us. Included, also, will be guides and an appropriate emergency support team. If you know of someone who might be interested, have them apply before August 31."

Something stirred inside of me. *This is a way you can get back into a more active outdoor life! But climbing mountains?* I wasn't too sure. I showed the letter to a couple of friends in the office. Some thought it would be a great adventure; others cautioned me against the dangers. I stuck the letter in my shirt pocket and tried to concentrate on my responsibilities of the afternoon.

That night I was restless. The Santa Ana winds blew hot off the desert and across my little island off Newport Beach. Throwing back the blankets, I tossed and rolled, knotting the sheet with my restlessness as new thoughts ricocheted off the walls of my brain.

I wondered what climbing the highest peaks would be like. Mount Whitney, Mount Hood, Mount McKinley—they were only words. What would they be like to climb? I knew they were dangerous for experienced, two-legged climbers.

Who do you think you are, even imagining such a thing? How could a leg amputee challenge those killer mountains? You must be insane to think that anyone could succeed at such a feat with only one foot!

My mind went back to the fateful decision that qualified me to consider the challenge.

Whether in Tulsa, Kansas City, or Salt Lake City, the beige walls of the doctors' offices looked the same. Each meant the same thing to me—hope followed by disappointment. And here I was again, sitting on the edge of the examination table in a skimpy examination gown waiting for the physician's return. Idly, I rubbed my inflamed leg and gazed at the customary poster on the far wall, the one that illustrated the structure of the human leg and foot.

How many times in the last seven years have I sat like this, waiting for the results of further tests, X-rays, or cultures taken on this dumb foot?

Forced to leave college due to the infection, I landed a well-paying job as a petroleum land man and met Claire, the cutest little southern gal in the world. The only drawback was that Claire lived six hundred miles away in the state of Kentucky.

As I traveled with the petroleum company, I attended many churches. For the first time, I really studied the Bible. My relationship with God was stronger than ever during this time. Only my foot continued to hamper my life. Since the accident, I hadn't gone a week without having a sore somewhere on my leg.

My right leg was paralyzed below the knee because the propellor cut the sciatic nerve. So I couldn't feel any pain there, but an infection continued to fester. It always started inside my heel, a blue-black blood clot under the skin, the size of a silver dollar. When I walked, the skin would break, and I would leave round rings of blood behind, on the floor, in the shower, in my bed.

The wound refused to heal. Then, as the infection crawled up my leg, it attacked the lymph nodes. The swelling and pain spread into my thigh and groin. My ankle remained perpetually swollen from the ulcer. Constantly hurting, I found it difficult to maintain a positive attitude about life. And this had been going on for so long, I couldn't remember what it was like to be cheerful.

Sitting there in the doctor's office, waiting again, I remembered the time when I was sixteen and went hunting with my dad. We traipsed through the woods all day. When we got home, I hauled off my muddy boots to find my right sock red with blood and muddy with dirt. On closer inspection, I discovered a building nail protruding through my boot and sock straight into my foot. I had apparently walked on it all day without feeling a thing.

This time, I'd had it. I'd been sick with high fevers from the infection in my heel for the last time. I'd spent my teen years in and out of hospitals in attempts to stop the infection. I knew my foot was literally killing me, an inch at a time. I looked down at my flaming appendage and sighed. "It's now or never, God. This can't go on any longer."

The door opened, and Dr. Roger Emerson walked into the examination room. He sat down on the physician's stool and told me the results of the tests. "We can take skin from your shoulder and try to transfer it onto your heel . . ."

I began shaking my head before he finished making his suggestion. "No. No way! I've gone a similar route before, and it didn't work. What if we just treat the infection and don't do anything?"

"It will continue to spread, Todd, into other bones in your body." He frowned and wagged his head slowly. "There's no skin on your heel. It's exposed muscle. The bone will continue to chip off, causing more infections. You are already enduring excruciating pain in your upper leg and groin. It can only get worse."

I frowned and considered his warning. I had flown all the

way to Massachusetts General Hospital in Boston to see Dr. Emerson. He was one of the country's foremost orthopedic surgeons. My Uncle Bill, a retired colonel from the United States Army, had suggested the medical center as a last-ditch effort to save my leg.

"If we amputate the leg, will it take care of the infection?" I asked slowly.

Dr. Emerson examined my foot once more before speaking. "Yes, I think so. The infection is all in the lower part of your leg." He pointed at the inflammation. "That would take care of the infection."

"Fine! Let's do it!" I sounded more confident than I felt. *What would life be like without the leg? How would I manage?*

The doctor cocked his head to one side. "Just like that? Amputate? Are you sure you don't want to think about it first?"

I shook my head emphatically. "That's all I've been thinking about for the last two years."

"It's not a procedure that can be reversed, you know."

"I understand that, sir. I also know that my God wants me to be healthy. And I'll never be healthy as long as I keep having these infections."

He looked relieved. For once, he didn't have to convince a patient that amputation was the best treatment. This time there wouldn't be a long wait during which the patient deteriorated and finally became too weak to have the surgery.

"All right, then. We can schedule the operation for tomorrow if we can find you a room." He scribbled something on my chart, then looked up. "Why don't you get dressed while I have my nurse make a few phone calls."

I dressed with eager anticipation. Finally, something was going to be done. No more infections and no more fevers. I knew my strength would return. I hurried out to the waiting room to tell my uncle and my dad.

"Are you sure you want to do this?" my father asked.

"Absolutely. Now, just pray that they can find an available room for me."

Before long, Dr. Emerson appeared. He looked grave.

"Oh no," I groaned, "don't tell me I'm going to have to wait."

"Not necessarily." The physician paused, then continued.

"I found you a room, but I'd like you to see it before we actually check you into the hospital. It's in the old wing."

"Great!"

"Well, let's go take a look before you get your hopes built up too high," he cautioned. "Remember Mass General is an old hospital—it's been around for a very long time. And the available room is located in the oldest part of the complex."

The doctor led the way. I listened while Dr. Emerson explained the surgery procedure and the recovery period. As we proceeded down the labyrinth of narrow hallways, we dodged ventilators, gurneys, and miscellaneous equipment. Nurses and other medical personnel rushed by in a hurry to get to where they were going.

Dr. Emerson paused to check the number over the doorway with the one on his clipboard. He gave me an "I told you so; don't blame me" look, then pushed open the door. He gestured for me to enter the room before him. I stepped into the room that would be my home for several weeks following the amputation.

Multiple coats of white paint covered the walls of the tiny cubicle. The window looked out onto red brick walls and a wrought-iron fire escape. Faded bedspreads, crammed close together military style, covered the two metal army cotlike beds. I gazed about the drab little room and sighed. *How can I cope with the emotional experience of having my leg amputated in such a dreary place?*

"Is this it, Doctor?"

"I'm afraid so, Mr. Huston, at the present." The doctor exhaled. "However, if you are willing to wait a month, I can get you into the Phillips House."

I shot him a quick look. "What's the Phillips House?"

He chuckled. "The Phillips House speaks for itself. Let me show you." The doctor led us from the room and back down the hallway. "It's all part of the same hospital. Wealthy people from all over the world come here for their medical needs."

After a long walk through a maze of halls, he led us into what seemed like an exquisite old mansion instead of a hospital. All was quiet. Instead of the bustle of people and equipment cluttering the halls, a calm pervaded the area. Our shoes clicked on the gray marble floors. Dr. Emerson smiled as I entered a large room with its plush, upholstered easy chairs and an expensively draped oversized bed. Wallpaper covered the walls. Opposite the foot of the bed was a large brick fireplace with a Persian area rug in front of the hearth. I strode over to the window, pulled back the flowered drapery, and glanced out at what seemed to be a park.

Doctor Emerson stepped up behind me. "That's the Charles River. See those boats? Harvard rowing teams. Follow it out and you'll see MIT, Harvard, and Cambridge."

Turning slowly, I let the drapery drop back into place. "I think I want to wait for the surgery, sir."

"Are you sure you want to wait thirty days?"

My uncle, a former army colonel, spoke in a low voice to my father. "Tell him to stay in the other room."

"No." I shook my head emphatically. "I've been in and out of hospitals for seven years. I know how important my attitude will be to my healing. I'll do better if I wait."

The doctor agreed. Later that day, my dad and I flew home to Tulsa to await the required length of time. Over and over, during those thirty days, I questioned the wisdom of having my leg removed. I reminded myself that there'd be no going back, no way to reattach it if I changed my mind. *Maybe God will heal me miraculously. Maybe I'll awaken one morning with a brand-new, healthy foot. Maybe medical research with come up with an alternate solution.*

"Dear God," I prayed, "if You save my leg, I promise I'll never sin again. I'll become a preacher. I'll—I'll . . ." I bargained with every advantage I had. As the month drew to an end, I realized I had to make my decision on the facts as I understood them, not on a possible miracle or a wish. I knew things couldn't go on as they were. If I must sacrifice one portion of my body in order that the rest could live, I would do so. I chose a life and a lifestyle over a leg.

When it was time for me to return to Boston, I insisted that my parents should stay in Tulsa. "I can manage this alone," I assured them. "I know I'm doing the right thing. I'm giving up one part of my body to preserve the rest."

Reluctantly they agreed to stay home. As I kissed my mother

goodbye and gave my dad a hug at the Tulsa airport, they assured me that their prayers would go with me. All I could think of as the jet taxied out onto the runway was, *Finally I'm going to get rid of the pain and get rid of the infections. Finally I'll feel normal again.*

The night before the surgery, I checked into the hospital and was taken to the Phillips House as arranged. I'd prepared myself for a rugged night of tossing and second-guessing my decision. After the last medical attendant left me for the night, I got out of bed and walked to the window. Pulling back the drapery, I gazed out at the quiet spring night. Shards of light from a crescent moon glistened on the quiet surface of the Charles River. Beyond the park the lights from apartment buildings spilled out onto puddles of rain dotting the city sidewalks. Silhouettes of elm and maple trees touched the indigo sky.

"OK, God, You saved my life for a purpose. Will You help me now? Where are You in all of this?" I still harbored the thought I'd had since I was fourteen—maybe He'd heal my leg at the last minute.

While I sat there staring down at the cityscape, I could see the lights of Cambridge in the distance and the lights of Harvard and MIT in the foreground. I wondered whether Elijah had had similar feelings as he waited for God to speak to him on the side of the mountain. Would God speak to me through fire or through an earthquake? I gazed up into the clear night sky and saw no lightning and heard no thunder.

As I waited, not knowing what to expect, His power came to me, not through the touch of a divine hand reconstructing my leg or a dramatic intervention of nature's laws. He came to me in a whisper, like He did to Elijah.

A gentle rush of God's power filled me with peace and a knowledge that He would see me through the storm I faced in the morning. I felt His presence and His love. Though the outside remained the same, inside, I changed. Like a trusting five-year-old, I slid beneath the cool crisp sheets and fell instantly asleep.

The doctor scheduled my surgery as the last of the day so that any infectious tissue he removed would not accidentally contaminate other patients. The aroma of anesthetics lingered in the air as they wheeled me into the operating room. I'd arranged to be awake during the surgery with only a local anesthetic to deaden the pain. I'd had so many operations over the years that I hated the groggy feeling and the nausea that followed a general anesthetic. By the way they looked at me, I knew the medical team thought I was strange indeed to have made such a request.

"You know," I joked as the nurses hooked me up to the appropriate machines, "you should come down to my room after we get done here. I plan to order a giant pizza. They do deliver here in Boston, don't they?"

When the anesthetist rolled me onto my side and stuck the needle into my spine, I winced. The spinal block, while initially painful, would deaden the lower half of my body. I took a deep breath. If I'd had second thoughts, they were gone now. Slowly a tingling numbness traveled from my waist to my feet. I glanced up at the IV bottle beside me, then followed its drips to the tube that led to the needle in my vein.

One of the nurses checked the flow from the IV. "You must be crazy to do this awake."

"No, not really. I know I'm where God wants me to be, doing what He wants me to do."

I watched Dr. Emerson draw a map on my leg to indicate where the incision would be made. I glanced up at the person on my right side. Instead of a member of the surgical team, I imagined the presence of a giant angel standing beside me and shining down at me. Then they covered my face so I couldn't see the actual procedure and so that I would not breathe any of the germs from the rotting tissue.

This is it, I thought. *No going back now!* I felt gentle tugs as the doctor pulled on my leg muscles and cut through the tendons. Suddenly, the whir of the saw filled the room.

"This is insane!" The anesthetist stared down at my face. "Are you in pain?"

"No, I'm fine," I assured him. "God is taking care of everything." I glanced over at my heartbeat registering on the monitor. My heart raced, then settled down again. Feeling a little lightheaded, I closed my eyes to block out the glare from the light above the table. The doctors sewed me up, and the attendants prepared to return me to my room. Curious, I lifted my leg a little. It felt lighter than usual and shorter. When it dropped, it fell like a cannon onto the gurney. I glanced over at one of the attendants in surprise.

He grinned. "That's the IPOP."

I nodded. Before the surgery, the doctor had explained how they would wrap the stump of my leg in an IPOP, an Immediate Post-Operative Prosthesis, which would allow me to begin taking steps the very next day. The huge cast with the metal plate and the mannequinlike foot was designed to give an amputee a physical and a psychological advantage. I relaxed and watched the ceiling lights flash by while they wheeled me down the long, brightlylit corridor. As one of the attendants reached to open the door to my room, it flew open.

"Surprise!" My mother burst from the room, followed by my father. In his hands he held a giant pizza.

"Mom! Dad! What are you doing here? I thought we agreed you wouldn't make the trip."

My dad grinned. "You agreed. We didn't."

Mom kissed my cheek. "You don't really think we would have let you go through this all alone, do you?"

I smiled through a blur of tears. "Thanks," I whispered.

The next morning, before anyone instructed me to do otherwise, I decided to get out of bed and try to take a few steps. I had to be certain that I could walk again; I needed the security.

I sat up and swung my feet off the bed and onto the floor. I felt a little weak and dizzy. Slowly, grabbing hold of the bed with my free hand, I stood up and shuffled my feet forward two steps. "Aaugh!" I gasped from the pain that shot up through my leg, through my torso, all the way to the top of my head. All the pain I'd been through since the accident didn't equal the excruciating pain I felt taking those two steps. I dropped back onto the bed. "Oh, God! Will I ever walk again?"

CHAPTER FIVE

Pain and Possibilities

Los Angeles, California

The 50 Peaks Project was a plan to involve handicapped individuals in climbing the highest points in each of the fifty states. When I looked into it a little further, I discovered that there was a "High Pointers Club" of people who were working on this list of climbs.

Only thirty-one people had climbed all fifty high points. Needless to say, all of them were able-bodied, two-legged individuals.

Me, climb mountains? It wasn't so long ago that I had almost given up on ever walking again!

My body in agony, I pressed the Call button. *Hurry! Please hurry! I gotta have something for this pain!* Flames shot up my thigh and into my groin. The door opened. A pretty little red-headed nurse popped into the room. "May I help you, Mr. Huston?"

"I-I-I'm in a lot of pain," I gasped, wiping a layer of sweat from my brow. "I tried to walk and . . ."

She shook her head and clicked her tongue. "You should have waited for us to help you." She hurried to my bedside and helped me back under the sheet. "Now, if you'll stay put, I'll go see what the doctor has ordered for you."

I sighed and laid back against the pillow, shielding my eyes with my free arm. "Please hurry."

41

The pattern repeated itself day after day. Demerol, Percoset, Morphine, Perkoden, Tylenol with codeine, the brand mattered little, as long as it soothed away my pain. I had little choice! It was either the drugs or the agony.

I'd heard tales about people who'd gotten hooked on prescription drugs. And occasionally, I wondered, *Could such a thing ever happen to me?* I didn't want to explore the possibility too deeply, since I couldn't imagine enduring the pain without a shot of drugs to bring me sweet relief. And any concern I had about the possibility of being hooked vanished whenever a nurse handed me a small paper cup containing two little capsules. I tossed them into my mouth, gulped down the water, then waited for the promised relief.

Before leaving the hospital, I arranged to undergo a second operation to reconstruct my lip for cosmetic reasons and to repair the roof of my mouth to clear up a disorder in the tonal quality in my speech. I explained my reasons to the doctor. "Someday I'll be talking in front of large groups of people, and I want them to understand me." I never dreamed how God would make my prophecy come true.

When I was released from the hospital, Bruce, a good friend and my roommate from the University of Oklahoma, invited me, along with my little brother Scott, to stay at his parents' house in Boston until I completed the necessary outpatient visits. Scott had driven my car to Boston for me. He stayed once my parents returned to Tulsa so he could drive the two of us home when the doctor allowed me to travel.

I grew stronger and restless. During my weeks of recuperation, Bruce told us about the fun one could have living in Boston. One Saturday night the three of us attended a party at his friend's house. I wasn't sure how the women would relate to my having only one leg. It didn't seem to bother them.

When we left the party, we three guys climbed into my MazdaRX-7, rolled down the windows, and cranked up the stereo. We hadn't ridden far when we stopped for a red light and a brown Pontiac Bonneville, filled with college-age guys, pulled up next to us.

"Is that your daddy's car?" the guy on the passenger's side of the front seat yelled.

Bruce replied, "Is that your mama's car?"

"How'd ya like me to dent your car?" The driver of the other car revved his engine threateningly and snarled.

Bruce glared back. "How'd ya like me to dent your face?"

I stared at my friend in horror. "What are you doing? There are five guys in that car!"

Bruce ignored me. He eased the RX-7 into an empty parking lot. The other car followed, blocking our exit. The doors on both cars flew open. Eight men hopped out: five from their car and three from ours. I took a little longer extricating myself and my crutches from the RX-7.

I'd barely gotten to my feet when four of the guys lined up in front of my brother, Bruce, and me. Scott flexed and unflexed his fists, trying to look tough. Standing with my crutches, I gripped the hand holds so tightly I was sure I'd leave a lasting impression on the metal.

In the meantime, a fifth man circled around behind us, while the driver of the other car headed for Bruce. "I'll take this guy!" the driver announced, his body coiled and ready to spring.

Hey, wait! I thought. *This isn't looking too good.* I shot a glance toward Bruce in time to see him slam the driver in the nose. Blood spurted in all directions. The man's cry of agony spurred the other men to action. Two lunged at Scott, and the other two headed menacingly toward me. When I didn't see or hear any evidence of the cavalry galloping to my aid, I lifted my crutches to start swinging, Hopping about on my good leg, I tried to look dangerous.

Inches before reaching me, one of the two men stopped abruptly. "I don't want any part of this!" He batted the air in disgust and turned away.

"Me either!" The other man followed his example, as did the rest of the hoodlums, except for the one who had my brother pinned. I hobbled over to the two men wrestling on the ground and pulled the attacker off Scott. Before anyone else could react, I raised my crutch and slammed it down on the hood of their car.

"Now, get out of here and leave us alone!" I shouted, flailing my crutch in the air like a crazy man. They didn't wait for a second invitation. The last guy jumped in, and their Pontiac burned rubber out of the parking lot.

Since the three of us weren't injured, we climbed back into the RX-7 and headed for home.

"That was a dumb thing to do!" I growled at Bruce.

"Hey, they had it coming."

"You could have broken the guy's nose."

"Good! He had that coming too."

Ten minutes later, a police car motioned us to the side of the road. After going through the routine questions, one of the policemen asked, "Do you fellows know karate or what?"

"No sir," Bruce answered. Scott and I shook our heads innocently.

"Well, we had to take one of the guys back there to the hospital for stitches. You popped him a good one. You broke his nose."

"He deserved it," Bruce growled. "We were just protecting ourselves."

The policeman shined his flashlight in the back seat and spotted my leg, or the lack of it, and admonished us to be on our way. "And no more fighting!"

Bruce rolled up the window as the patrolman strode back to his vehicle.

"How could you say that you don't know karate?" my brother asked.

"Like we're going to tell the guy that we've all taken classes in karate? You want a law suit or something?"

"Hey," I reminded them, "they'd be laughed out of court once the jury took one look at my stump!"

"So, what's next on the agenda?" Bruce's eyes danced with deviltry.

I glanced at my watch and shuddered. "I think it's time we headed back to your house. Your folks will be worried."

"Yeah, you're right," Bruce admitted. "Let's go home and have a bowl of Friendly's ice cream. It's the best tasting, you know!"

I smiled to myself. *Good old Bruce, a great friend, if I can survive him.*

The month of recuperation passed, and Dr. Emerson released me from his care. We bade goodbye to Bruce and his family and started for home. The hot, humid summer weather stayed with us as we toured New York City and Washington, D.C.

As the RX-7 sped along the interstate across the central states, I glanced over at my brother driving my car. *I hope you know how much I appreciate you, little brother. I'd be helpless if I were alone and got attacked.*

On the way through Kentucky, we stopped to see my girl-friend, Claire. Five foot two, chestnut brown hair and eyes, she greeted us warmly. Before we arrived at the house, I fret-ted about her reaction to me after the amputation. I shouldn't have.

"I was in tears the whole day you had your surgery," she said. In spite of the medication I was on at that time, I re-member every detail of the few hours we enjoyed together.

The longer we spent together, the more I hoped to convince her to attend the University of Tulsa that fall. As we prayed together, we both agreed that we wanted to do what God had planned for us.

Upon arriving back home, I enrolled in fall classes. Due to finances, Claire chose not to attend the University of Tulsa that fall. We continued writing to one another, eventually get-ting engaged.

The doctors fitted me for my first artificial leg. The leg was heavy, made of hard fiberglass and wood. With a heavy rub-ber foot bolted onto the leg, it was rigid and cumbersome. I had to wear an elastic belt around my waist to help hold it in place.

For an active young man of twenty-one, the prosthesis was a torture to wear. It made me self-conscious. Not only did I detest the way it looked through my clothing, I hated the way it prevented me from doing all the things I loved most.

Uncomfortable and bulky, the prosthesis prevented me from taking more than four or five steps without feeling pain. Due to the discomfort of the fit, the stump would swell causing sores and blisters to develop. When I removed it, my prosthe-sis sock would be blood soaked. Then I'd be forced to go with-out the leg to let it heal.

After all I had been through, it was hard to take. *Did I go through the surgery only to suffer the same problems I had before? Was it all for nothing?*

The prosthesis made it difficult to concentrate on my class work. Life became unpredictable. I couldn't make any plans. I had thought the amputation would free me from all of this, that I would be free to live my life as I always imagined. Except for the lack of any further infection, not much had changed for the better.

In order to keep active, I would go to the gym and work out my upper body. But the pain and discomfort continued. Continued pain meant continued drugs.

Being hooked on the medications made my rehabilitation more difficult. I found myself taking drugs rather than doing the things I should be doing. I grew easily agitated and lethargic. Not only was I wasting away my life, but I was destroying the relationships that were important to me. Worse yet, I knew that living from one "fix" to the next wasn't God's will for me.

The use of prescription drugs intensified. I enjoyed the euphoria they afforded as well as the relief from pain. I found myself exaggerating the pain as an excuse to ask for more pain medications.

Mornings were difficult. I felt tired and lethargic. I lost what little enthusiasm I had for attending my classes when I discovered that the medicine had a greater effect when taken on an empty stomach. Sometimes I would take the pills every other day to increase their effectiveness. When I did this, I experienced withdrawal symptoms. I become nervous and shaky. Then I'd interpret this normal discomfort as a pain needing medication.

My parents watched and worried over my drug use. "Son," my father would say, "aren't you taking more medication than you really need?"

"No! You can't know the pain I feel or the amount of drugs I need to take!" I tightened my jaw in defiance determined to justify my behavior. "Besides, don't try to tell me if I feel pain or not. You don't know what it's like to have a leg amputated!" Then I would storm up to my room and nurse my wounded spirit.

I believed I was handling my needs well. I would hold off taking my medications until after the day's classes, and I'd be careful never to drive under the prescription's influence. My tolerance level for the medications increased, forcing me to alternate between the different prescriptions.

My eating habits became more erratic. I would go without eating for days to get an empty stomach so as to intensify my highs. Occasionally, I admitted to myself that I had a problem and I would try to stop, but inevitably, I'd return to the drugs within a few days, using them more heavily than ever.

Night after night, when I could sleep, I dreamed of a Kansas wheat field, with blue sky and a gentle rolling grass land, and I'd be running along a well-worn path that cut through the field, totally free of my artificial leg—no pain, no awkwardness, just totally free. But with the dawn came reality— I wasn't free; I would never be free.

Claire and I continued writing to one another and visiting when we could. I never mentioned the drugs I was taking except for those deadening the pain. We became engaged, but within a short time we both realized that the distance between Kentucky and Oklahoma made our courtship almost impossible to maintain. Without anger, but not without pain, we broke our engagement.

One summer day in 1984, I took four tablets of Demerol. Within fifteen minutes, my forehead and face felt numb. A buzzing sound commenced inside my head. My sight blurred. I could tell that I was slipping in and out of consciousness. I stumbled down the stairs to the living room, where my father was reading the paper.

"Dad." My tongue felt dry and cottony. "I think I OD'd on my pain medication. I think I'll call the pharmacist at the hospital for advice."

My father hovered over me while I placed the telephone call and explained what I'd done to the pharmacist. "What should I do? Come in and have my stomach pumped or something?"

"No, you probably are not in any danger from taking only four tablets. I say that cautiously, since every person is different." He warned me about abusing my medication, and I promised never to do so again.

Back upstairs in my room, I fell across my bed, burying my face in a bed pillow. "Oh, dear God, I almost blew it this time, didn't I? You know how many times I've vowed to quit using the stuff. But it never works. You know that I can't break this vicious cycle without Your help." Tears were coursing my cheeks. I'd never felt so helpless in my life. "Please, Father, if You will help me, I will stay away from all drugs."

Instantly, my mind cleared. The buzzing in my head stopped. All signs of drowsiness and lingering euphoria disappeared. I got up off the bed, collected the hidden half-empty bottles of medication, and placed them in the medicine chest in the bathroom.

I won't say that I never desired the medications again. And I won't say the pain in my leg miraculously disappeared on its own. But I can say that day by day, God gave me the strength to resist. A month later I swore off all other drugs, including aspirin, alcohol, and caffeine. Except for occasions like a sprained ankle or a wisdom-tooth removal, I've never returned to them.

It wasn't long after that that I heard about an amputee's ski clinic at Tahoe, California. My family encouraged me to attend. I resisted at first. I didn't want to hang around with disabled people. I wanted to be seen as "normal." The idea of spending a week with fellow amputees, all discussing their aches and pains like little old ladies in a sewing circle, sounded boring. But reluctantly, I agreed.

Was I in for a surprise! Nearly one hundred people of all ages attended. I was assigned a roommate named Steve. Steve had lost his arm in a washing machine accident. We had the greatest time learning to ski. And I made many great friends. By the end of the week, my attitude about disabled people had changed. I discovered them to be like everyone else. While they had disadvantages due to their injuries, these people had learned to love life. I was chosen, along with Lori, a beautiful, blue-eyed young woman, to be photographed on the chairlift for the promotional material.

I went home from California with a new attitude. The wooden prosthesis continued to bother me, but I went on. Whenever I walked even a few steps, I would experience pain. I enrolled in graduate classes at the University of Tulsa and finished my undergraduate degree in finance.

After graduation, I crisscrossed the country, picking up jobs here and there in California, Texas, and Tennessee. Still restless, I headed to California for graduate school. I'd decided to study to become a psychologist.

There I met and fell in love with Jessie, a captivating young woman from New Zealand. After only three months of dating, the subject of marriage popped up. A brisk December wind whipped about us as we sat on a rock at the beach watching the surf break on the shore.

"Todd, I heard from immigration today about my visa." Jessie drew imaginary circles on my pant leg.

"Oh?"

"My visa is about to expire. They're going to send me back to New Zealand."

"No!" I drew her into my arms as if to protect her from the possibility. I loved Jessie. The thought of her being an ocean away from me terrified me. I didn't want to lose her, because of the distance between us, as I had Claire, "There must be something we can do."

"If we got engaged . . ."

My heart leapt at the idea. *Marriage! That's the answer.*

The week before Christmas, we flew to Tulsa and got married in my parents' home. From then on, I worked harder than ever at my studies, as well as holding down a job in the psychiatric ward in a local hospital. During exam times, I would go as long as thirty-six hours without sleep.

Second semester came and went with the usual work, classes, friends, and fun. We'd been married but a short time when Jessie began chiding me about my missing leg. Day by day, she chipped away at my self-esteem. She complained that I kept her from being as free and active as she'd like to be. It was like a knife cutting out my heart every time she whined, "We can never go with the gang when they go surfing or camping or any of the fun things most young couples do."

At first, we attended church together. This had been important to me during our courtship. I believed she had the same goals as I did. But soon it became apparent that our dreams were poles apart. A year into the marriage, we hit a major snag. Jessie admitted to having had an affair.

"Why, Jessie, why?"

"Well . . ." She hesitated before driving the knife into my heart. "I guess I liked the freedom I have with him. It sounds silly, but he can run and carry me in his arms, things you will never be able to do." Somehow, we picked up the pieces of our relationship and promised one another to work at making our marriage a success.

I graduated with my master's degree in psychology and found employment as a psychiatric assistant in the children's psychiatric ward at a local hospital. While the job didn't pay much, I enjoyed working with the children, helping them face the problems in their lives.

Jessie belittled my new position and the amount of money it generated. Living in Southern California was expensive. Each month it took our combined checks to survive. As her two-year temporary immigration status passed, Jessie became more and more restless.

"If you would quit your job and look for work up near Hollywood, I know that I could find work in the movie industry. That's always been my dream, you know. That's why I came to the U.S. in the first place." Her petulant little mouth quivered; her clear green eyes filled with tears.

I reached out to her to gather her in my arms. She resisted. I sighed. I wanted to be supportive. I had tried to catch a glimpse of her dream since the first time she voiced it. But I loved my job and I loved living on Balboa Island.

Most of all, I dreaded the possibility of losing the one with whom I'd chosen to spend the rest of my life.

CHAPTER SIX

Dreams of Running

Talkeetna, Alaska

As soon as I stepped out of the bunkhouse, I searched for a glimpse of Denali. But the great mountain remained hidden behind a curtain of mist and clouds.

I thought back to the day I had first heard of the 50 Peaks Project. I wasn't sure I would ever hike again, much less climb mountains. I had come so far . . . would my hopes, my dreams be shattered in disappointment again?

The loaded van sped down the Pacific Coast Highway. "Do it again, Mr. Huston. Do it again!" the children shouted. "Take off your leg again." The driver of the van laughed as the children begged me to remove my artificial leg.

We'd enjoyed a great day at the beach, but I had been hurting most of the day from the small particles of sand that managed to creep in between the prosthesis and my stump. So when we loaded the van for our return to the adolescent psychiatric hospital, I unfastened my artificial limb. The kids shrieked with delight when I allowed them to take my leg and hang it out the van window for drivers of the passing vehicles to see.

I liked working with the children. Many of the rewards were instantaneous. My wife didn't. Jessie wanted to leave the hospital's employ and move closer to Hollywood.

"But I'm doing what I feel God wants me to do," I answered.

"God?" she fired back, "He doesn't care about us!"

I was shocked. "What if you have to answer to God for what you are saying?"

"I don't have to answer to anyone!" She snorted in derision.

Her vehemence disarmed me. I thought I'd married a woman who was spiritual, who believed in God like I did. With the continued pressure, I relented. I agreed to quit my job and move to Hollywood. I gave a two-week notice on our apartment.

One evening, as I prepared to attend midweek meeting at the church, I asked Jessie to go with me. She hadn't attended church for some time, and I was concerned. I noticed that she seemed agitated and nervous, but I didn't give it much thought, since Jessie was often restless.

"Are you sure you won't go with me?" I asked.

She shook her head. "No, I'd rather not."

"Well, do you want me to stay here with you?"

"Oh, no," she answered hastily. "I'll be fine, really."

"OK." I kissed her on the cheek and left. "We'll spend some time together when I get home, OK?"

"Sure."

I enjoyed the service and headed for home in a pleasant state of mind. When I parked our car in front of our place, I thought it strange that all the lights in the apartment were out. I climbed the stairs and unlocked the front door.

"Jessie? Jessie?" *Maybe she's asleep,* I thought. I expected to hear the television going and to find her curled up on the sofa, but all was silent. I tiptoed into the living room, hung up my jacket, and immediately sensed something was wrong. The sound of my footsteps echoed off the walls as I crossed the room and peeked into our bedroom. The bed was gone. I flipped on the light and gazed about the room. The sliding closet doors yawned dark and empty where her clothing had been. Framed photos, her perfume bottles—missing. Her dresser drawers were on the floor, bare and abandoned. On the desk, I found a note. A lump grew in my throat as I read her message.

"Dearest Todd, I'm sorry, but I'm so confused. I need to get away for a while to do some thinking about us and our relationship. I hope you can find it in your heart to forgive me."

The paper flitted to the floor. I reached down to pick it up and noticed that the top drawer of the desk was partly opened. I opened it the rest of the way and discovered that our checkbook was missing. Our sheaf of monthly bills was still there, but the checkbook was gone. I rushed through the apartment, searching for traces of Jessie. Only the aroma of her perfume lingered to remind me of her. Dazed, I sank onto the sofa.

I couldn't believe it. She was gone. She'd stayed with me long enough to get her green card, a permanent visa that didn't require she be married. I buried my head in my hands. "Oh, God! What next? This is more than I can bear!"

Suddenly I felt claustrophobic. I had to get out. I couldn't stand being alone in our apartment. It held too many painful memories. Everywhere I looked, I saw Jessie. I grabbed my sweater and charged into the night. *Where does this leave me? What should I do?*

I wandered down along the shore. The water gently lapped the wooden pilings of the docks. The stars stood out in bold relief against the moonlit sky. The bells on the sailboats in the bay tinkled lightly. The lights of the city dotted the hillside behind me. I had never felt so alone before in my entire life.

It was as if I were a desert island, totally isolated and empty. In my misery I cried, "Oh, God! What am I supposed to do now? She wanted to live near Hollywood, so I gave up everything for her. Now I have no job, no place to live, and hundreds of dollars of bills to pay. What is it You wanted for me?"

Day after day, I looked for work. Night after night, I walked down to the dock and stared out over the water, until the pale shades of dawn appeared behind the eastern hills. Then I would trudge back to the apartment, shower, and go job hunting again. One night, after a particularly despairing day, I sat on the pilings at the bay silently listening to the night sounds around me. I had passed the point of demanding answers from God. Like Elijah, I sought an answer. I had run ahead of God before with Jessie. This time, whatever I chose to do, I would wait to hear God's will.

Then it came to me—work with amputees.

"Amputees, Lord? How can I make money working with amputees? There's no money doing that. I need money to survive!"

Again, I heard the message, "Work with amputees."

I couldn't deny the message. I had to submit. "You know that wherever You are is where I want to be. I made that promise a long time ago, and I've kept it. It's not always been easy, but I've kept it."

Taking a deep, ragged breath, I whispered, "OK, Lord. If You provide me with the opportunity, I'll do the work."

That decision settled some of the jangle in my brain. Only the emotional pain was left. I prayed that God would heal my emotional scars. "If Jessie is gone for good, help me to forgive her."

A refreshing peace swept through me. I leaned back and gazed at the stars over my head, at the clouds, at the moon—an artist's canvas of constant motion. It was as if the heavens had opened up and I knew without a doubt that God would create everything I needed to make His plan happen for me.

A few weeks later, I learned that my wife had flown home to New Zealand and returned to the States without telling me. About the same time, I found employment with NovaCare—the largest artificial limb company in the world. I started as the clinical director of their Amputee Resource Center, visiting recent amputees in the hospital and teaching health-care professionals about the psychology of amputation. I traveled to Washington, D.C., for the Amputee Coalition of Amercia, to negotiate with senators and congressmen about improving the health care of amputees.

With my financial prospects back in order, I again focused my attention on my failed marriage. Friends encouraged me to have Jessie arrested for fraud and deported. I contacted her and told her about my new job working with amputees.

Her answer—"There's no money in that! Be a man and get a real job."

Our topic of discussion turned to her departure and her citizenship status. "You know, of course," I reminded her, "I could go to the authorities and have you deported."

"You try that and I'll lie!" The cold steel in her voice chilled my heart. "If you ever come back at me, I'll tell such whoppers of lies about you that no one will ever believe you again."

I hung up the receiver, discouraged and heartsick. *How could the woman I love become so vicious toward me? When did her heart harden,* I wondered as she continued her tirade about me and my new position. *Did she ever really love me?*

I rubbed my upper leg. It had been a particularly difficult day, and the artificial leg had opened old blisters on my stump. *If she did love me, when did she turn away from God, and from me?*

Now that I was working full time again, I considered the possibility of getting a new prosthesis, a lighter one that would allow me more maneuverability. Since my surgery at twenty-one, I'd worn a wooden leg. The prosthesis was heavy and cumbersome, making it difficult and painful to work or to walk. I had broken it several times, so it looked like the sidewalk in front of my office—cracked, but repaired.

Reading my employee benefits package, I discovered that the company's insurance benefits would pay up to one thousand dollars for an artificial limb. I needed a new one badly. My eight-year-old prosthesis had been broken and repaired so many times, I wasn't sure how much longer it would last.

I began shopping around for a new one. The best deal I could find would cost me fifteen hundred dollars above the insurance's portion. I didn't have that much. In fact, I didn't have any money since Jessie had virtually emptied our savings account. I couldn't afford to buy the leg, nor could I afford to go without it. So I took my problem to God.

"You know, Father, that I can't afford this expense. Yet, if I don't have it, I can't work and make a living. Please help me to know what to do."

About the time I finished the paperwork necessary for ordering the prosthesis, my employer switched insurance companies, forcing me to begin the entire qualification process again. I also learned that neither company would pay for the type of leg I really needed.

After months of negotiating for the artificial limb that would be best for me, the new insurance company agreed to pay for a carbon graphite leg. Unfortunately, this leg wasn't the one my physician recommended or the one I felt I needed. It kept breaking in half whenever I placed the least physical demands upon it. With it, I couldn't be any more active than I had been with my old prosthesis.

About this time, a friend of mine prodded me into attending some meetings at a business convention in Irvine, California. In the course of the meetings, the fifty people attending were divided into groups of five. Our group found a quiet spot and formed a circle. Three of the members of our group worked for PacifiCare, the insurance company providing coverage for my employer. In fact, Jeff Folick, the president of PacifiCare, was part of my group.

The group leader restated the purpose. "We're supposed to take turns answering two questions: how do I want to be seen by other people and for what do I want to be remembered."

One by one the members of our group introduced themselves and answered the questions.

"I'd like to be remembered for helping abused children."

"I'd like to be remembered as fostering world peace."

"I want people to remember me for my community service."

When my turn came, I began, "I think it's great what each of you have said you'd like to be known for. But I think it's important to take the philosophy and apply it in the workplace. For example . . ."

I told them my story of trying to get the leg the doctors recommended and not being able to because the one I needed cost relatively few dollars more. "The one I got took seven months to get fitted and has broken twice in the short time I've had it. Now, I'm only one person with a problem. But each of you encounter many people just like me every day. If we can take our high ideals and use them to solve or to simplify the lives of those people coming to us, we'll have accomplished our goals—even if we don't achieve world peace. At least, our corner of the world can be more humane and caring."

When I finished speaking, the president of the insurance company said, "I want to talk with you about this."

By 10:30 the next morning, I received a call from his organization. The representative told me, "You got the leg you want. Get started immediately with the fittings. We'll pick up the cost."

I could hardly believe it. But immediately I could see God's hand in bringing Jeff and me together. The Flex-foot Reflex VSP was everything I'd hoped it would be. I took my first steps. It didn't hurt. It was made of lightweight material with shock absorbers built in so that my stump didn't need to take the abuse it did with the other prosthesis. I could move about more freely and less painfully.

For the first time in seventeen years, I began to hope that my recurring dream could come true. Maybe it would be possible one day to run across a grassy field, not in Kansas, but on Balboa Island.

My joy faded whenever I thought of Jessie. Now, I could be what she claimed she wanted in a husband. *No,* I told myself. *This leg wouldn't make a difference to her. She won't be truly happy until she's happy with herself. Face it, Todd; your marriage is over. It's time to face it. It's time get your head together. God has given you a chance to do the things you really want to do. Get busy serving Him.*

There I was, at thirty-one years old, wanting to learn to run again. I hadn't run since I was fourteen. Talking with amputee friends who regularly ran made me believe my goal was achievable. *If they can do it, so can I.* I was determined. Able-bodied jogging friends encouraged me as well.

The fog rolled back in off the Pacific the morning I gazed down the beach, ready and eager to begin my first run. I took a deep breath, stretched, and swung my arms from side to side. I felt exuberant and alive. I didn't want to overdo on my first time out, so I decided I would run the circumference of the island once and quit.

I charged down the pathway, then moved to one side as an older woman jogged by me. We waved at one another. I ran a hundred feet, then collapsed against a fence.

My breath came in short, painful gasps. Sea gulls overhead mocked me with their calls. I couldn't believe it. My legs refused to cooperate with one another. They kept hitting each other, causing me to trip and my weight to shift. I was afraid I would topple onto my face.

I stumbled to an empty bench and sat down, my head buried in my hands. *Oh, God, am I trying to do the impossible?*

Have I received the leg too late in life? Am I trapped forever, never to realize my dream of running? The athlete who could outrun and outmaneuver his opponents on the playing field in junior-high was embarrassingly uncoordinated. I stumbled back to my apartment, disappointed.

All I wanted to do was crawl back into my bed and bury my head. However, since I'd told so many of my friends I was beginning a running program, I couldn't hide from my defeat.

"Quit? No way! You're not a quitter!"

When I complained about my weakness to the older woman who jogged by me earlier, she laughed. "Hey, that's the way it is for two-legged runners too, you know. We stumbled over our own feet and ran out of breath when we first started too."

Alone that night, I remembered the trials I'd already been through: the accident, the many surgeries, the drug addiction, the long, painful recoveries, my wife's chidings, and our subsequent divorce. *Now, those were mountains, Todd,* I told myself. *Learning to run again is kid's stuff in comparison.*

Yet the image of myself tripping over my own feet, trying to run, taunted me. All the demons of insecurity rattling around my brain mocked my dreams. I knew I had to run. Running would be overcoming a psychological barrier as well as a physical one. If I were ever to experience my dream of being active, hiking and camping, doing all the things I'd enjoyed as a kid, I had to begin with running. If I stopped trying now, I would probably remain sedentary the rest of my life—always dreaming, but never doing.

The next morning, I strapped on my new leg, tightened my shoelaces, and adjusted the sweat band on my forehead. I jutted my chin forward. *"I'm going to do it, Lord. I'm going to do it."*

As the early-morning fog lifted over the ocean, I set out running, stumbling, walking. I determined to go the hundred feet again. I'd only run a few feet when Eleanor, the older woman, jogged past.

"Keep at it," she called over her shoulder as she disappeared around the next bend.

I persisted. For a week I ran the hundred feet. The next week I doubled the distance by running the first one hundred feet, then walking the second. But it was a strain. Every morning, as Eleanor passed me, she called out encouraging words.

After a month of running every morning, I completed the circle around the island for the first time—1.6 miles. Totally winded, my legs like rubber, I limped back to my apartment and called my parents to share the thrill of my accomplishment. They tried, but they couldn't understand why I was so excited. My local friends understood more how I felt; but even they couldn't fully comprehend what that 1.6 miles meant to me.

I continued running every morning, farther and farther. One morning as the sun cleared the tops of the coastal range, I decided it was time to fulfill my dream. I would run the dusty trail across two miles of field grass, not in Kansas, but in the back bay between Balboa Island and Newport Beach.

Up and down, across the gentle hills, I charged. That day, I outran my heartaches, I outran my pain, I outran my loneliness and my fears. It was as if I'd been released from a maximum security prison. No walls were too high; no bars too strong to hold me now. I knew that God and I could do anything.

In three months' time, I extended my run from Balboa Island to Laguna Beach, twelve miles up and down hills, without stopping.

My next goal was to go kayaking on the ocean. Since I'd maintained the strength in my upper body, I found the days out on the ocean refreshing and invigorating. The rowing strengthened my cardiovascular system. I then added hiking and mountain biking to my list of sports. The trails in the hills around Laguna Beach gave me plenty of exercise in the early mornings and on weekends.

My new agility set me to remembering the good times I'd had camping as a Boy Scout, then as an Eagle Scout. I decided that I wanted to start camping again. However, I wasn't certain I could lug all the necessary equipment on my back while maneuvering the rough terrain.

My first visit to a camping supply store in seventeen years delivered quite a shock. I couldn't even identify half of the equipment being sold. I did recognize the exorbitant prices, however. Reluctantly, I sighed and left the store. Camping with such pricey gear would have to wait. *Maybe in time,* I told myself. *You still have your kayaking and running.*

About this time, the letter about the 50 Peaks Project arrived. Something stirred inside of me. *This is a way you can get back into a more active outdoor life! But climbing mountains?* I wasn't too sure. I showed the letter to a couple of friends in the office. Some thought it would be a great adventure; other cautioned me against the dangers.

All fifty high points had been successfully climbed by thirty-one persons, none of whom were disabled. I knew I wanted to go, but I was scared, scared I might fail. I had experienced enough failure—my leg, my marriage—could I handle another defeat?

But haven't I learned that God and I can overcome any challenge? Still, where would I even start? What would I need for supplies? What kind of a workout program would I need to get into shape for such a climb? Is this God's plan for me?

Throughout that long, restless, night, questions raced through my mind. *Is this the opportunity I prayed about on the dock the night Jessie left me? Could God be planning to work through this challenge to bring glory to His name?*

The squawking of gulls searching for their breakfasts could be heard over the bay before I fell into a deep sleep. Like everything else, I knew this was better left in God's hands. My last thought was a prayer. "God, I don't know if You want me to do this or not. If You do, let everything work out. If not, I'll be happy not to pursue it further."

CHAPTER SEVEN

Fifty Peaks—On My Own?

Talkeetna, Alaska

With a warm breakfast in my stomach, I sat in the ranger station along with other hopeful climbers and watched a National Park Service video on Mount McKinley.

When the film credits finally rolled, I glanced out the window at the overcast cloud bank that separated us from the famed mountain. I still hadn't caught a glimpse of the Great One.

A park ranger strode to the front of the room and turned to stare at us. Finally, with a solemn face, he asked, "Do you really want to go on the mountain? One bad step—" he waved his index finger in front of our faces—"one bad step, and it's over!"

He paused to let his words sink in. "It might be on an ice fall. You might break through a crevasse and slide down the side of the mountain beneath the surface of the ice. You could disappear ten feet from your tent. It could even be an avalanche."

Fragments of information raced through my mind. A snow avalanche can uproot whole forests, tumbling pine and fir as if they were matchsticks, rolling huge boulders before it, spewing tons of snow, rock, dirt, and trees into the valleys. Slides have been known to flatten large buildings like a tractor might crush a Big Mac carton. John Muir told about a snow slide in the high Sierras that wiped out an entire lake, taking water and fish with it.

The ranger continued. "It may be a glacier—on those, one misstep and a man can disappear forever." He paused and eyed each one of us, as if recording our faces for future identification should the need arise.

"Returning climbers are reporting winds strong enough to brush a man off the side of the mountain. And then there are possible whiteout conditions when you can become disoriented and freeze to death."

By now, my teeth chattered and my insides rumbled like one of the mountain's own rock slides. I tried to calm myself before my breakfast made a return appearance. *The man must be exaggerating.* I had been told how rangers will discourage people from climbing the mountain. They figure, if someone does decide not to climb, they should never be up here anyway. *How bad can it really be?*

Even as I considered the possibility, I knew we weren't listening to Stephen King horror stories here. The tales he told were all too true. *So, why in heaven and earth are you subjecting yourself to such dangers? Who do you think you are? Some rough and tumble guy who eats nails for breakfast? Todd, how did you ever get yourself into this?*

I will fill out that application, I decided the next morning as I ran. I realized that even considering such a plan meant that I had to get my body into the kind of shape it had never been in since the accident, seventeen years ago. My survival would depend on just how well I trained. I felt as if I would have to prepare for battle, a battle against my body as well as my mind.

During lunch, I filled out the application and dropped it in the mail slot. I spent the rest of the day trying to push thoughts of the expedition from my mind and concentrate on performing my daily routines.

After all, I reminded myself, *maybe I won't be chosen to go, maybe the application will get there too late to qualify, maybe God doesn't have mountain climbing in mind for me.* Over the next few days, during idle moments at work, while running in the mornings and falling asleep at night, I thought about the climb and hoped and prayed for God's will to be done.

The more I thought about it, the more I decided that I needed advice, expert advice. I called my friend, Fred Zakolar. Fred lived in Reno with his wife Kathy, another good friend from Oklahoma days. I read the letter to him over the phone. "I'd like to do it, but I'm not sure I'm able. I'm just beginning to learn what this new leg of mine can do."

"I think you should go for it, Todd," he encouraged. His confidence in me meant a lot, since I knew he would never urge me to do something he didn't think I was capable of doing.

"I don't know that I'll even get chosen, but if I get picked to join the team, will you help me out?"

He answered immediately. "Of course, Kathy and I'll do everything we can to help you, Todd. You know that."

Four days later, a packet arrived in the mail from the 50 Peaks Project. I stared at the return address, almost afraid to open the envelope.

"That doesn't look like a rejection letter." Pat, one of my co-workers, examined the package. "It's too thick."

I sent a quick prayer heavenward and ripped open the envelope. A letter fluttered to the floor. I bent down and picked it up, took a deep breath, and began to read.

"Dear Mr. Huston:

"We are glad to inform you that you have been selected to join 50 Peaks Project's expedition." The letter spelled out the financial and legal obligations, as well as other bits of information I would need.

"I'm going!" I shouted, giving Pat a high five. "I'm going! I've been asked to join the expedition!"

I read through the letter again, letting the words sink into my brain. This was for real! "Man, I've got a lot to do to get ready!" Immediately my mind set rolling the game plan that I'd developed while waiting for the letter. I was bursting with ideas. I knew I needed to learn about mountaineering as well as get into shape.

"I'll need to join a gym. I can increase my endurance by working out on the treadmill and maybe, the StairMaster."

"You know," Pat volunteered, "the club I belong to has a rotating rock wall that works something like a treadmill."

"Great! Sign me up."

The rest of the afternoon I found it impossible to concentrate on the work stacked on my desk. My mind kept wandering to the subject of the anticipated climb and all I had to do to prepare to go. I put a call through to the director of the 50 Peaks Project. I had a thousand questions to ask. He had one or two of his own. "Do you know any serious mountain climber who might be consider being one of our guides?"

Immediately I thought, Fred. *If Fred's along, I know we'll have a great time.* Fred agreed to be a part of the team.

I had a difficult time explaining it to my folks. My mother worried about my physical safety, and my father was concerned about my financial well-being.

"You just got a new job, son. You can't take time off to climb mountains."

Their anxieties were valid. Since receiving the letter and seriously considering doing it, the logical side of my brain had thought of little else. I continued to counsel with friends and co-workers.

After Jessie walked out on me, I'd joined a singles Bible-study group called the "Becomers" at the Newport Beach St. Andrew's Presbyterian Church. That week, I attended the regular Tuesday-night meeting. As pumped up as I was about the climb, it took a miracle to help me concentrate on the evening's lesson. Yet I knew I needed spiritual energy during the next few months as I prepared for the climb.

I told the members of the prayer group about the 50 Peaks Project. "There will be an asthmatic, a young man with multiple sclerosis, a blind woman, another woman who is seventy years old, and then, me, an amputee. I need to train for this. So I wondered if any of you might be interested in hiking with me."

A young blond woman named Lisa volunteered. After the meeting I told her to meet me at my home on Balboa Island, and we would hike the cliffs of Corona Del Mar together. We quickly became friends. Lisa's cheerful nature and upbeat attitude made the climbs fun. In addition to our regular climbs, we talked long hours on the phone, sharing what was going on in our lives.

Because of the prayer group, she knew about Jessie. And I knew how she'd been a computer graphic artist for Apple Computers. Burned out on corporate life, Lisa had recently found work in the Huntington Beach area as a textile designer.

It was great to have someone with whom I could share the excitement of my new job at NovaCare Orthrotic and Prosthetics. When I had a presentation to make at a seminar for health-care workers in La Jolla, Lisa attended. Afterward, she had some great ideas for strengthening my presentation.

Yet, despite the different areas of my life smoothing out, I couldn't let go of the memory of what Jessie had done to me. A raging desire in me wanted her to pay, and pay good. I had the law on my side. I could get her expelled from the country. The officials would never even grant her a visitor's visa in the future. However, such a prosecution would take an enormous investment of my time, energy, and money. *Is my anger strong enough?* I asked myself. *And if I put so much time, energy, and money into getting my "just deserts," what would I have left to prepare for the big climb?*

I realized that over the next few months, I could choose to use my time, my energy, and my money to prosecute Jessie and have her deported, or I could use that same time, energy, and money to prepare for the climb. To do both would take away from each. I wanted to go on the climb so badly I could taste it, yet, letting go, doing nothing to the woman who'd trampled on my trust, my self-confidence, and my good name—I wasn't sure I could do that.

One evening I tried to sleep, to forget, but the war raged inside of me. Frustrated, I trudged down Coral Avenue once again and sat on the dock, watching the phosphorescent waves dance in the moonlight and listening to the bells on the sailboats ring in the wind. *Which will it be?* I asked myself. *The mountain or revenge?*

Again in the stillness of the ocean breezes, I could hear my God saying, "Todd, leave her alone. She's mine. I'll deal with her."

Just let go? Walk away? "But, Lord," I cried, "it's not fair! She shouldn't be able to get away with what she's done!" My heart rebelled at the very thought. Again the message came to me.

"Let her alone. She's mine. I'll deal with her."

Again I beat my head against the idea of "letting go." But finally I did. I left her and what she deserved in God's hands. I made my decision—the mountains.

Once I turned Jessie and my thoughts of revenge over to God, once I let go and focused my thoughts on preparing for mountain climbing, I had more energy than I would have believed possible. I called Fred and asked him for an exercise routine that included running, biking, kayaking, and weight lifting. He faxed one through immediately.

For the next few months, my heart raced and I'd feel faint and out of breath on my morning runs before going to work, but I kept running. After eight hours at work, I exercised on the treadmill, the StairMaster, and on the rotating rock wall, then went home to body surf on the ocean in the evenings. Weekends, I hiked in the mountains around Southern California and rode my mountain bike in the hills outside Laguna Beach.

Autumn gave way to winter. I received word that the 50 Peaks Project would be having our first meeting as a team in Provo, Utah. I flew to Fred's place in Reno. The night before we drove to Utah, we watched *K-2*, a movie about mountain climbing. My mouth hung open through the whole movie. As the credits rolled by, I turned to Fred. "No way! Not me!"

He laughed and told me not to be such a wimp.

The organizers of the climb supplied us with the necessary information and stressed the need for more financial backing for the project. We posed for photos with the other team members, then headed west toward Reno.

"Ya know, Todd." Fred tapped his fingers on the steering wheel. "I've got a bad feeling about this."

"I know what you mean. I wonder if 50 Peaks can actually pull this thing off."

"You know," Fred suggested, "it wouldn't hurt to have an alternate plan just in case everything falls through."

"What do you mean?"

"Would you want to climb the fifty high points on your own?"

I thought about his suggestion for a moment. "I don't know."

"We could raise the money we will need for 50 Peaks while we're working on a backup plan."

"Hmm, that's a thought. I wonder if my company would consider sponsoring me?" I thought about the possibility the rest of the ride back to Reno, then again on the flight back to California.

When I talked with the company executives about sponsoring the 50 Peaks Project, they voted to donate five thousand dollars to the cause as well as give me the leave of absence I needed to do the climb.

The holiday season came and went, and I hadn't heard from anyone at the 50 Peaks Project. In January I called them. They had no progress to report. I went out to dinner that evening with Lisa. I told her how some of the 50 Peaks investors hadn't come through.

"I guess I have to make some tough decisions. Should I continue with my dream or let it go? I really believe God led me into this and that He has big plans for me."

Lisa looked across the table at me and matter-of-factly said, "Then you need to do it. I'll be behind you all the way." She added, "You should seriously consider beginning a journal. If this thing is as big as you believe it to be, you'll want to keep an accurate recording of the day-by-day preparations."

The next day Lisa showed up at my apartment with a black leather diary.

A few days later I talked again with the 50 Peaks director. Things didn't look much better than they had earlier. I placed the receiver on its cradle and stared idly out the window onto the quiet little back street in front of my apartment. The row of weather-beaten houses clung together like a line of fading chorus girls. I rubbed the back of my neck and left shoulder. "What now, Lord? It isn't looking good, is it?"

Feeling frustrated, I called Whit Rambach, one of the guides for the project. I asked his opinion on the situation. Whit's thoughts echoed mine—not good. "Todd," he reminded me, "you have the money for your climb. I'd be glad to forget the group and climb with you. When you decide, let me know."

"Right. I'll do that. And thanks, dude."

I strolled into the kitchen and grabbed a glass of water, drank it, then paced back to the living room, then back to the kitchen, pacing out my troubled thoughts. "Todd, do it on your own!" A familiar Voice spoke to me.

I stopped. "Do it on my own?"

"Todd, do it!" I didn't hear a voice, just an impression inside me that God was giving me divine permission.

A rush of excitement flooded through me—a feeling of completeness, even though it hadn't yet begun. I darted to the telephone and called Fred in Reno. In detail, I told him the latest on the situation with the 50 Peaks Project. "I don't think they'll be able to do it."

"I've been expecting that," he admitted.

"Let me ask you a question. If I decide to climb the 50 peaks on my own, will you . . ."

Anticipating my question, Fred interrupted me. "Absolutely! Whatever you need! Just let me know how I can help."

I smiled to myself. *That's Fred,* I thought. Knowing I had his support encouraged me. We talked a few minutes longer about the preparations I'd need to make for an independent climb, then signed off.

"I'll get a list of equipment that you'll need to you by the end of the week."

"Thanks, man."

"Hey, no problem. Let me know if there's anything else I can do to help."

Then I knew it for sure. *I'm going to climb mountains!*

CHAPTER EIGHT

Summit America

Talkeetna, Alaska

The look on the ranger's face left no doubt in my mind. He knew that someone in that room was going to be injured or killed on the mountain.

Once again, a familiar thought pummeled my brain. Was I using the climb as a distraction from the pain of the divorce? Or trying to prove to myself that I could do anything a two-legged man could do? *No!* I reminded myself. *God and I have settled those issues. I'm here for God and the message He wants distributed to His children!*

"Any questions?" The ranger seemed to be staring directly at me.

"Yeah," a climber behind me drawled, "when do we leave for base camp?"

A nervous chuckle passed among the first-timers.

The ranger eyed the man, his countenance grim, yet professional. "According to the weather service, we will need to wait for a break in the clouds up on the mountain in order to facilitate a safe takeoff and landing."

"How long can that take?" another hiker asked.

The ranger shook his head. "Your guess is as good as mine. The Great One operates on her own time schedule, not man's."

I called Lisa and told her about the decision to go on my own. "I think I can do it," I said. "I think I can set a new world record. I think I can even beat the record set by a nonhandicapped person."

"Hey, you know I'm behind you."

"I'll need help back here," I confessed. "I was thinking of asking you to operate the business side of the climb."

"Sure," she said, "what do I have to do?"

With my friends so willing to help me, I knew my chances for success were much greater. When I told the people at work about my change of plans, I heard everything from, "We wish you the best," to "Forget this harebrained scheme, Todd. It ain't gonna work!"

Yet inside my heart I knew God wanted me to do this. And if I worked hard, it would happen. Whit and I worked out our plans by telephone. He drove down from Fresno to help finalize the logistics of the climb.

To help finance the project, I contacted potential sponsors— $5,000 here and $3,000 there; a hundred here, five hundred there. The North Face and REI, large suppliers of hiking gear and outdoor wear, agreed to give me a discount on equipment bought at their stores.

Hoping for another donation, I explained the change in plans to my employer, but he refused. However, the company worked with me, redesigning my leg so it would stand up to the abuse it would get hiking across glaciers and up boulders.

Amputees can't normally do what I proposed. A regular artificial limb only gives back to you 20 to 30 percent of the energy that your real leg gives. NovaCare's Flex-foot helped replace the natural spring in one's own leg. I also glued the sole of a boot to the bottom. This way, I didn't need to wear a boot—and that kept it light.

Roy Snelson, the director of Wings of Calvary, a Christian nonprofit organization that provides artificial limbs for people in Third World countries, also contributed to the climb. He said, "If God wants you to climb, He will provide."

The climb began to take over my life. I woke up at 6:00 a.m. and planned until I had to leave for work. From 6:00 to 8:00 p.m., I worked out. After that, I planned until late—often to

1:00 or 2:00 a.m. Asleep or awake, my mind raced. *What should I be doing next? What am I not doing that I should be doing? What do I need to know? How am I going to do everything on time?* To find peace and comfort, I turned everything over to God—again and again and again.

Both at work and in preparation for the climb, a whole new world opened up to me. I found myself talking with business executives; being interviewed on the news and on local talk shows.

"Why are you doing this?" they would ask.

"I just want to show that people can overcome whatever obstacles they face in life," I explained. "It's more than just climbing mountains—it's about dealing with whatever life hands you. With faith in God, you can make it happen!"

Then I would explain the business side of the climb, that this wasn't a wild-eyed project without planning and hope of succeeding. God gave me the words I needed to convince people to take the risk and put their money on me.

It was happening. It was really happening! That week Whit, Lisa, and I formed our own climbing expedition under the name "Summit America."

Lisa got busy developing a marketing plan for "Summit America." The first thing she needed was a promotion logo. So she, Whit, and I sat around my kitchen table, doodling, trying to come up with an appropriate logo for our new venture. After hours of drawing, we went over to a Mexican restaurant on the island. And on one of their napkins, we came up with a design we all liked.

Lisa went directly home from dinner and created the logo on her computer. The next day we ordered 144 T-shirts to be printed up. We decided that Whit and I would sell them around the country as we climbed to earn more money for the project.

Quitting her job at the textile company, Lisa decided to go "freelance." This would give her more time to do the everyday things in preparation for the climb. There was so much to do and so little time in which to do it. I poured over the High Point guidebook, trying to decide where to start and how fast we had to move in order to set a new record.

A few nights before I left on the first climb, Lisa and I walked down to the dock. Standing at the end of the pier, we prayed together. We both knew how important prayer was for the success of the venture.

We weren't only praying for the success of the expedition. We were praying for my safety. Everywhere we went, people offered to pray for me. Deep down, I feared for my life, especially on McKinley. When I shared these thoughts with Lisa, she quietly assured me, "God has been in this thing right from the beginning. I know He'll carry you through safely to the end."

As Whit and I prepared to leave, a newspaper reporter from one of the newspapers Lisa had contacted did a story on the climb. The Orange County Network Television and radio station KNX 107 in Los Angeles did the same.

The front page of the Metro section of the *Orange County Register* carried our story the day we set out on our journey. Lisa was so excited that she bought sixteen papers for all her family and friends.

On our way to the airport for our flight to Oklahoma, we heard my voice on the radio, discussing the climb. As I settled into my seat on the plane, I recalled the events of the past few days. At that point, I felt physically, psychologically, and spiritually prepared for the climbs. I actually thought I would get a chance to finally relax.

As long as I stayed focused on God and His plan for me, I knew I could succeed. Getting on the plane had been but another step of faith in a journey that had begun months earlier. With just that step, we had gotten farther than most expeditions.

At my folks' home in Oklahoma, we put a camper shell on Dad's red Ford pickup and loaded up our supplies. With a final goodbye, Whit and I began the adventure of a lifetime— maybe.

The official clock for the record would start on the summit of the first high point and end on the summit of the fiftieth one. To break the record, we had to climb all fifty in less than 101 days.

Heading north, we began a drive that would take us to all forty-eight lower states, over twenty thousand miles. Our first high point was in Nebraska.

The open fields and fresh air set the mood for a glorious beginning: buffalo grass waving in the sunlight; carefully defined fields of early wheat; endless, cobalt blue skies fading to the horizon. Nebraska's Panorama Point, although not very high, was aptly named. From that simple summit, we began our quest.

Next, we traveled north toward South Dakota's 7,242-foot Harney Peak.

Outside Hot Springs, South Dakota, the sky darkened. Rolling black clouds billowed in the sky. Thunder roared; bolts of lightning shot across the sky, illuminating the terrain in a ghostly light.

Whit peered out at the approaching storm clouds. "Looks like we won't be sleeping outside tonight."

Lightning flashed too near our vehicle for comfort. "Probably not," I muttered.

During my years in Southern California, I'd forgotten what real thunder storms were like. Then the rains came, thunderous, pounding rain. Our windshield wipers fought to keep ahead of the downpour. We drove slowly, following the dotted white line down a corridor of pine trees. Granite rocks jutted out from among the trees. I rolled down my window and inhaled the clean pine scent. "I love it!"

By the time we pulled into the Harney Peak trail-head parking lot at Sylvan Lake, the rains had slowed to a drizzle. I spied a rainbow forming in the east. I leapt from the car and scanned the patches of blue sky above the peak. "Do you think we should risk it?"

Whit grabbed his backpack from the back of the truck. "Sure, why not?"

I strapped on my waist pack, grabbed my walking poles, and headed down trail number nine, breathing in the clean, clear air as I walked. With the smell of rain heavy around us and the wind whistling through the trees, I felt great! At first, the trail was muddy, but the ground quickly absorbed the rainwater. Whit and I began to establish a climbing routine. He liked to climb solo, so he would either go on ahead or hike a ways behind me.

Hearing someone approaching from behind, I turned, expecting to see Whit catching up with me. Instead, it was another climber. We introduced ourselves. He commented on my artificial leg. I told him about my goal to climb all the high points in the United States.

We talked as we hiked. I asked him about himself and what he did for a living.

"Right now?" A dullness washed over his eyes. "Right now, I'm nothing. I'm trained as an engineer. And up until a few months ago, I worked for a major chemical company back east." He kicked a pebble out of the pathway. "The stress got to me and I burned out. So I stored my stuff in my dad's garage, and here I am."

He talked about the hiking he'd done and thoughts he had on reentering the job force. "Out here on the trail, all those monstrous problems don't seem so important, do they?"

I laughed. "It's amazing how insignificant day-by-day problems become when you're concerned for your survival."

He chuckled. "Yeah, I guess so." We hiked together for a time; then I hurried on ahead.

Whit caught up with me at the top of the peak. At the base of the stone lookout tower, we read the plaque honoring Dr. Valentine T. McGillycuddy, the first white man known to reach the summit. We shot some photos of beautiful scenery—rocks jutting out of the pine forest—from the top of the tower. Two young women traveling home from the West Coast stopped to talk.

"We decided to get back to a more normal lifestyle than we were living in Southern California," one of the women explained.

I agreed. "I know what you mean. It seems that no matter how well off you are or how successful you might be, you're always just breaking even."

Then Whit and I hiked back to the car, and we headed north to Rapid City. Suddenly, Whit burst out laughing. "Look at that!" he said, pointing into a field.

There sat a kitchen stove with its oven door wide open and a sign next to it that read "Open range."

Again, the torrential rains fell. We arrived in Bowman after 11:00 p.m. It had been a long six hundred miles since five that morning. We found a hotel and checked in for the night.

In the morning we climbed White Butte—North Dakota's high point—3,506 feet. The rains of the night turned the trail to a muddy, slippery, soggy mess. But again I was impressed with the solitude I experienced on the mountain.

We returned to the town of Bowman, cleaned up, ate lunch, then headed south toward Iowa's unnamed high point—1,670 feet. When we stopped for lunch, I called ahead to ask permission of the farmer who owned the property. I took an extra moment to explain who I was and what we were doing. "So you won't mind us trespassing on your property?"

"Of course not. It's no problem," the owner assured us.

"We'll be coming in quite late tonight," I warned.

"That's fine. We enjoy high pointers. And we wish you the best."

I thanked her, hung up the phone, and we headed south once more. Whit and I took turns driving while the other slept. I drove through quiet little towns and vast fields of grain. While I drove I reviewed our progress. *Only two days, and we've checked off five high points. That's good. And when we hit the eastern states, we'll be checking them off even faster!*

I slowed the truck to a stop near a farmhouse. In flat states like Iowa, the high points were often less than impressive. In pitch darkness, we hiked up the slight slope between the farm buildings to the water trough. I felt goofy standing in the middle of a barnyard in the middle of the night, having my picture taken. But there on the trough roof was an Iowa license plate—HIGH PT.

We considered throwing our sleeping bags on the ground and sleeping right where we were but decided to drive farther north to a KOA campground in Minnesota.

At 3:00 a.m., we pulled into the campground, located a camping spot, threw our bags on the ground, and slept. At six the next morning, after a shower and breakfast, we loaded our gear and drove east toward Minneapolis. Turning north onto the Lake Superior Highway, we appreciated the tranquil blue water on our right and the rolling green hills on our left.

We battled an infestation of mosquitoes in order to summit Eagle Mountain—2,301 feet high—the highest point of Minnesota. The marshes and ponds of the Boundary Waters Ca-

noe Area, formed by the spring runoff, provided the mosquitoes with a perfect breeding ground. And we provided lunch!

We had to walk across boards laid down over the water, so
there was no escaping the bugs. We walked as fast as we
could.

The bug spray I used for protection proved to be more of a
threat to me than to the bugs. That night, when I was trying
to fall asleep, I found it hard to breathe, like I was having a
panic attack. The next morning I awakened jumpy and lightheaded. And I still had a hard time breathing. My throat was
swollen. So were my ears—they looked like cauliflower. After I
drank some water and took a shower, getting the spray off my
body, I felt much better.

We were surprised to meet one high pointer along the way,
carrying an ice ax. Why he'd carry an ice ax when there was
no possibility of snow, Whit and I couldn't imagine. The swarm
of mosquitoes constantly circling our heads discouraged us
from talking for very long. We sped back to the truck, only
stopping to take a couple of photos to record the climb.

From there we headed for Duluth. Driving along Lake Superior toward Michigan's high point, Mt. Arvon—1,979 feet—
we could trace thunderstorms as they crossed the lake. Mt.
Arvon is located on the state's upper peninsula.

We parked the truck, then hiked along a logging road to the
top instead of over the trail. We got to the top and took pictures, though there was no vista to photograph, since the
foliage on the trees blocked all views as well as the sunlight.

Interestingly, Mt. Arvon was just recently named as
Michigan's high point. Two other mountains had previously
held the title. More modern surveying efforts were changing
geography lessons in this state with several mountains of
nearly the same height.

If another mountain was named high point before we finished our fifty climbs, we would have to come back to Michigan and climb again.

Next was Wisconsin's high point, Timms Hill—1,951 feet.
There we climbed the lookout tower and watched an orange-
and-red sunset with a young couple who had been hiking
behind us. I shared my personal challenges and goals with

them, and they did the same with me. They were just finishing college and had dreams of starting a family someday.

"Don't let any challenges hold you back," I urged. "With faith in God and in yourselves, you can overcome anything."

Whit and I rose early the next morning and headed south past dairy farms and green pastures to the Wisconsin-Illinois border.

As we passed a county fair in southern Wisconsin, I wished I had time to stop and stroll along the midway of spinning rides, screaming teenagers, hucksters, and junk-food stands.

But we had high points to scale and a record to break. We stopped to sleep in the small town of Scale Mound. Finding a Little League ballpark, Whit unrolled his sleeping bag on the top of a picnic table, while I slept on the grass in left field.

I climbed into my bag, folded my arms in the back of my head, and gazed up at the myriad of stars overhead. *If I tried this in the bigger cities, I'd get mugged. What an all-American place to sleep!*

CHAPTER NINE

Mosquitoes, Gnats, and Toenails

Talkeetna, Alaska

The stories I had heard tumbled around in my mind as I left the ranger station. *I have to hope I can make it. I've got to give it my best shot. I've come too far to wimp out now.*

I called Lisa to check on last-minute arrangements for media coverage. The media was an ally to get the message out. And we knew that the maximum press coverage would bring the financial rewards our sponsors expected for investing in the project.

"An NBC/CNN news team will document your landing at Kahiltna Glacier," she assured me.

"Great!"

"Well, I guess I'd better go help with the equipment. We have to be ready the minute the weather breaks." I paused, reluctant to break the connection with my friend and business partner and with the sane and familiar world of Southern California.

Lisa sensed my reluctance. "You be careful now, you hear?"

"You too. After all, more lives are lost on the San Diego Freeway each year than on Mount McKinley," I teased.

"Not in snow avalanches or hidden crevasses, though," she quipped. As we said our goodbyes, I could sense that her thoughts matched mine. *Maybe forever . . .* I waited for her to hang up; then I hung up my receiver.

Phone calls to Lisa had been a big part of every day's climb. One of the most exciting ones came that first week.

"Todd, you're not going to believe this!" She was so excited, I thought she'd leap through the phone lines. "I want you and Whit to put your ears to the phone. You know how I told you about setting up a T-shirt stand on Coral Avenue here on the Island? Well, yesterday, after sitting there for fifteen minutes with no sales, I prayed, 'God, I'll stay here five more minutes. If You want me doing this, let me sell some T-shirts in that time.' "

She stopped to catch her breath. "Immediately a couple came by with their three-year-old daughter and bought three shirts. And just as I put the couple's shirts in a bag, an older man jogged by. Noticing the stand, he turned to see what I was selling. You're not going to believe it, Todd!"

I could picture her eyes dancing with excitement.

"I told him about you and how you want to let people know that through faith in God and in the abilities God gives you, you can overcome whatever challenges you may face in life. The man asked me how much money it would take to complete the climb. I told him what you told me—twelve thousand more dollars."

"And? And?" I couldn't believe she was taking so much time to say what she wanted to say.

"And, the man said, 'Call 1-800-ABCDEFG tomorrow and ask for me. I'll write you a check.' "

"What?" My voice must have scaled from bass to high soprano.

"I couldn't believe it. I asked him if this was for real. He assured me it was. The couple who bought the three shirts had witnessed the entire conversation. The man interjected, "Congratulations. You just made a $12,000 sale!"

I sat stunned, with the receiver glued to my ear.

"So today, I contacted Mr. Shanahan as he asked. Within an hour, he had me in his office, asking for details on the climb. After I explained it all to him, he pushed the button on his intercom. 'Sue, make out a check to Todd Huston for $12,000.' Within minutes, I had the check deposited into the account!"

"So who is this guy anyway?" I asked. The phone number seemed strangely familiar.

I heard a delightful giggle at the other end. "The CEO and founder of *Hooked on Phonics*. Mr. Shanahan lives right here on Balboa Island. Can you believe it?"

I could hardly believe it, but when I got off the phone, I had a special praise and thanksgiving time with God. Once again He had supplied just what I needed, just when I needed it.

Curious cud-chewing cows lined the fences as we trudged along the dirt road to Illinois's high point, Charles Mound—1,235 feet. The high point sits on the border between Wisconsin and Illinois. In the days of the pioneers' trek west, the White Oak Fort, located on Charles Mound, protected the Kellogg Trail, an old stagecoach and wagon route.

We walked up the driveway to the farmhouse to find the owner of the land around the high point. A dog rounded the corner of the barn, barking. An older woamn in a housedress and Mother Hubbard apron opened the front door. The dog growled, then hid behind her skirts.

I thought, *That dog's in for a surprise if he bites my leg.*

She watched me through narrowed eyes as I explained our purpose for being there. "All we really need is your permission to walk across your land to the marker where we'll take a few pictures to record that we've been here. Then we'll be on our way."

"It'll cost you five dollars—for upkeep and all."

"Upkeep?" I couldn't imagine what there was to keep up. Not wanting to waste time discussing the matter, I reached into my pocket for a five. She took the money, stuck it in the pocket of her apron, and scurried back inside the house, taking the dog with her. When the door closed, I heard a definite click of the lock.

I turned to Whit and grinned. "Obviously she's not into high pointers, huh?"

He scratched his head and smiled. "Guess not."

We climbed the gates, dodged through cow dung, and ran past a group of tombstones—lost graves from covered-wagon days—to the high point. After taking the necessary snapshots, we hurried back to our car and headed south and east toward Indiana's unnamed high point. It sat in the middle of a field, marked with a small rock cairn and a steel pole with a sign attached reading, "Indiana's High Point—1,257 feet."

Then it was on to Ohio and Campbell Hill—1,549 feet high. We parked at the Highpoint Church and hiked about a half mile to the middle of the schoolyard of Hi-Point Joint Vocational School. Except for a group of boys bullying a smaller boy, the kids were gone for the day. We found the gate to the fenced-in yard, walked up the hill to the flagpole that marked the high point, and took our pictures.

From Campbell Hill, we headed toward 5,344-foot Mt. Marcy, the highest point in the state of New York. We spent the night near Cleveland, then drove through a corner of Pennsylvania and up to Niagara Falls. In spite of our rush, we took time to tour the falls. I'd seen them before, but Whit was amazed at their size. We read about people who rode the falls in barrels. *And I thought we were nuts!*

Clicking off the miles along the New York Turnpike, we turned north from Syracuse toward Watertown, then east along Route 3 through the hills of Adirondack High Peaks Region. We drove the last several miles to the Mt. Marcy campground in a drizzling rain.

Our guidebook told us that the mountain's Indian name is Tahawus, meaning "cloud splitter," and that in 1901, Vice President Teddy Roosevelt rushed down the mountain when he learned that President William McKinley had died.

Though it was late when we arrived, we stopped at the Adirondack Mountain Club lodge. We asked the ranger on duty about the climb and about a place to sleep.

"It's a strenuous hike," he warned. "Fourteen point eight miles to the top."

I asked him about the trail. "Just how long will it take to climb to the summit?"

"Well, that's hard to tell. If you find you're only partway up the mountain and half your day is spent, you'd best turn around and come back down."

"That didn't answer my question. If you're worried about my artificial leg, you should know that we're out to set a new high point record. We're on our way through the eastern states before we climb McKinley." I didn't mention that one of my toenails was black from an earlier climb.

"Oh, well, then I guess Marcy won't be that big a challenge for you fellows. You might want to watch out for bears, however."

"Bears? What do I do if I meet one? Climb a tree?"

The ranger chuckled. "Make a lot of noise. They'll run away."

The next morning I led the way up the Van Hogenburg Trail, and was quickly out of sight of Whit and the truck. I chatted with a number of day hikers that I met. Along the wide, well-marked pathway there were lean-tos and rest areas. At all the campsites we passed, people's food was tied up in trees—to keep the bears away.

After a few miles, the trail became rocky and steep. It split in various directions, one way for hikers and other ways for cross-country skiers. As the route grew more rugged, I began to worry that perhaps I'd taken the wrong path. The next blue mileage markers reassured me that I was still on the correct trail. The mileage remaining to the summit did not encourage me—7.4 miles. This was the longest one-day hike I'd ever done. I worried that my toe and foot might not hold out.

I crawled up dry creek beds and crossed rushing streams. I hopped from boulder to boulder, hoping I wouldn't fall and break my prosthesis. It was rough going. The idea that I could fall and I'd be stranded along the trail until someone came along frightened me.

I stopped to rest beside a waterfall, made beautiful by the spring runoff. Whit caught up with me, and we climbed the last distance to the summit together in fog and drizzle. At one point, my worries came true. I tripped over a rock and fell face first. Instinctively, I threw my hand out in front of me to stop my fall.

When I opened my eyes, a jagged rock was poised two inches from my nose. I was grateful that Whit was with me at that point.

A stiff, chilling wind blew on the summit. *Sure glad it's not winter,* I thought as I tightened the drawstring of the hood to my nylon jacket. Massive cloud formations billowed above our heads as we huddled beneath a couple of giant boulders to pose for pictures.

Worried, I eyed the storm clouds blackening the sky. "We'd

better hurry back and drop below this."

My stump throbbed from the long climb. I stopped to rest, to relieve the pressure and to allow blood to circulate through the area. This caused a burning sensation that felt like sandpaper on an open wound. I talked with other hikers as they passed, massaging my swollen limb all the while. From there on down, every half mile or so, I had to stop and loosen my artificial limb in order to let the blood circulate again.

Whit caught up with me at one of the lakes. After checking to see that I was all right, he kept on going. I hiked on, counting each step and mentally dividing the steps into miles to the camp. The last mile felt like ten miles, but finally I came to the end of the trail and the parking lot where we'd left my dad's truck.

Exhausted, I found a pay phone and called Lisa. I got the answering machine. At the beep, I said, "I am so sore! This is what I sound like after a fifteen-mile hike!"

A long, hot shower soothed my leg and restored my spirits. I felt good about being able to make such a long hike. However, I knew it was nothing compared to what waited out west. The ranger invited us to a barbecue that night, but we had to refuse. We still had a long drive to Vermont's high point, Mt. Mansfield—4,393 feet.

After a heavenly stay at a fellow climber's bed-and-breakfast, we drove to the Mansfield trail head. Grabbing our jackets and water packs, we hiked up the 1.4-mile trail to the summit, swatting huge flying bugs and pesky gnats with each step.

Along the way, I had a great conversation with Patty, a nurse who, like me, was going through a painful divorce. She'd married an alcoholic without knowing it.

"It devastated me."

I nodded. "I know how you feel. That's exactly how I felt after Jessie left. But, you did everything you could—don't blame yourself. If it's any comfort, in the long run, you'll be a lot better off."

She grimaced. "I know. However, right now . . ."

We hiked off the mountain together. I wished her well and left for Mt. Washington in New Hampshire. By the time I found a phone and called ahead, the toll road up the mountain had closed for the day. When the ranger heard what we were doing, he offered to get us a special pass. "Be sure to come by the office to pick it up when you arrive," he cautioned.

For many miles before we reached the base, we could see the impressive 6,288-foot mountain. Occasionally a cloud would obscure the peak. From the guidebook I read that weather fronts often collide at the summit. Because of that, the mountain is considered dangerous by hikers everywhere. In 1994 alone, five people died hiking Mt. Washington.

Because of the lateness of the day, we chose to drive the narrow, winding toll road instead of hiking the summit trail or riding the cog railway. Sheer dropoffs prevented us from driving too fast. The rules of high-pointing do not require a person to hike to the marker if a road is available.

On top, overcast skies and blowing winds urged us to hurry with our photo taking. We could only faintly make out the buildings on the summit. After checking out the tram, the oldest cog railway in the world, built in 1869, I wandered into the lodge and toured the restaurant and gift shop.

From Mt. Washington, we drove to Maine and Mt. Katahdin—5,268 feet. Climbing Katahdin's strenuous three-and-a-half-mile trail would be, like Marcy, a one-day climb. Baxter Peak, on Mt. Katahdin, is the northern terminus for the Appalachian Trail, which runs from Maine to Georgia.

We found a place to park by a lake and decided to sleep there. We threw our sleeping bags on the ground and sacked out for the night. Then the gnats found us.

Buzzing in my ears, crawling across my forehead, crawling into my nose, the pesky little creatures persisted in spite of the mosquito netting covering me. In desperation, I threw my stuff in the truck and stalked over to a bathhouse, where I sat, my back against the wall, and slept as best I could while Whit slept in the truck's cab.

We hiked the Appalachian Trail early the next morning. Swarms of mosquitoes took over where the gnats left off the night before. Hill after hill we climbed, sometimes steep, sometimes gradual, until we broke into the clearing above the timberline. We hiked up steep boulders to get over a rock ledge and onto a large plateau, all the way swatting at swarms of militant bugs. Stinging black flies, a cross between a mosquito and a horsefly, bit through our long-sleeved shirts. Their bites drew blood and left huge, painful welts on our arms, legs, and necks. We continued to wear our heavy shirts despite the ninety-degree temperatures. Finally, we summitted.

Whit looked around, then growled, "Fine! We made it. Let's take the pictures and get out of here!"

"Let's do it!" Sweaty, thirsty, exhausted, with streamlets of blood running down my good leg, my ears, and my neck, I continued swiping at my attackers. "This is miserable!"

He hauled out the camera from his pack. "This has to be the worst climb of the entire expedition!"

"I agree!"

On the way back down the mountain, I stumbled onto the secret for warding off Maine's insect population. I soaked in every stream I crossed. Once I was drenched, the bugs left me alone. I felt so refreshed that I thought I'd found the fountain of youth.

By the time I climbed into the truck at the trail head, I ached all over; one toenail was turning black; my stump throbbed from the pain; my ears had swelled to the size of Dumbo the elephant's—thanks to all the bug bites—and I was so thirsty I thought I'd pass out from dehydration.

Outside the park, we stopped at a little general store for cold drinks. I considered walking over to a pay phone to make a call, but I didn't have the energy. I couldn't feel my toes. The ball of my foot ached. And my stump felt as if someone had stuck a thousand needles into it. While Whit was in the store, I removed my prosthesis and turned the heater in the truck to high. I'd discovered that in lieu of a soaking bath, the heater eased the pain in my stump.

Whit came out to the truck and opened his door. A gust of hot air blasted him in the face. "What? Are you crazy? I can't believe that you have the heater on in ninety-degree temperatures!"

"The heat helps. It really helps."

He climbed into the truck, rolled down his window, and closed the vents. "OK . . ." he wiped the sweat form his brow, "guess I can survive the heat until we find a suitable motel."

I could barely walk from the truck to the office by the time we located a motel. My artificial leg off, I hopped from the office to my room. Once inside the room, I called Lisa, then my mother. When I told my mother how much my left foot was hurting, she urged me to have it X-rayed.

"You might have broken it," she warned.

I looked down at the blackened toenails, one barely hanging on.

"Please, Todd, go see a doctor."

Whit drove me to a hospital in Bangor, where I asked for an X-ray. The nurse on duty in the emergency room asked me how I'd managed to injure my foot so badly.

"Climbing mountains."

Her eyebrows arched in surprise. "Mountains?"

"Yep." I grinned. "My buddy and I are out to break the current record for climbing the fifty highest points in the United States in the least amount of time. And we have a good chance of doing it if I haven't messed up my foot too much."

"Isn't it a little unusual for a man with your disability to climb mountains?"

"That's the whole point. I want to prove that the challenges in one's life do not need to keep you down. With God's help and your own determination, you can do whatever you set your mind to. Of course," I added, "no one ever said it would always feel good."

She smiled, nodding her head as I spoke. "That's terrific, Todd. So many people come through this hospital, despondent and giving up on life. I'm glad to meet someone who doesn't allow their limitations to keep them from pursuing their goals."

The X-rays came back a few minutes later. Everything looked fine, except for the blackened nail dangling from one toe. I knew the nail would continue to be a problem. It would need time to heal before I tried to climb the western states.

"I hope this works," I said to Whit. Taking a paper clip, I straightened the wire, heated one end with a cigarette lighter, and cut the nail off the toe.

He shuddered. "That's gross!"

Good thing he wasn't around for my amputation. I sacrificed a leg to save my life—losing a toenail to save the climb was no big deal.

CHAPTER TEN

Delaware Danger to Texas Heat

Kahiltna Glacier

The wings of the red Cessna 172 dipped low over the Kahiltna Glacier as our pilot prepared to land on the wide-open glacier field at the base camp. Crevasses lined the edge of the landing area. The plane's skis scraped over the icy surface as we skated to a stop. Adrian tapped me on the shoulder and pointed out his window. "There she is."

Stunned and wide-eyed, I pressed my nose to the window glass like a kid gawking at a traffic accident from the safety of his parents' automobile. The mountain dominated its surroundings, as gigantic and as beautiful as I'd believed it to be. A large lenticular cloud engulfed the summit. My heart raced. *What a place to die!* I closed my eyes for a moment to steady my thoughts. *Get a grip, Todd; have faith. Have faith!*

I checked my watch, tapped it, then shook it again. 5:15 p.m. *Could it be so late?* We'd spent much of the day waiting for the weather to break so we could land on the glacier. This was our second attempt. Due to the heavy cloud cover, the pilot had been forced to return to Talkeetna, where we waited for a window in the storm front before returning. Finally we got the break we were waiting for, and we were on our way once more. *This is it,* I thought. *This is truly it.*

Tents surrounded by ice walls clung to the glacier like tiny colonies in a filmmaker's image of another world. Climbers bustled about the base camp in the evening twilight, making last-minute preparations for the grand adventures that would come with the morning. A group of climbers, their sunburned faces tired and worn, their beards scraggly, stood at the edge of the landing field waiting to board the plane and head for home.

Every glimpse I caught of the majestic mountain triggered a sense of awe within me. We'd climbed some impressive peaks already, but this was the big one, the big daddy. Mount McKinley separated the serious climbers from the Sunday strollers.

The pilot landed the plane and taxied across the runway to where a cluster of people waited. Immediately I identified the NBC/CNN news team Lisa had promised would be there. As the propellers whirred to a stop, I adjusted my sunglasses, took a deep breath, and pasted the confident publicity smile on my face.

Someone opened the door and I stepped gingerly out onto the snow runway. Gingerly, since on the flight up, the pilot had shared a story about someone who had stepped into a crevasse right on the airfield and disappeared.

A brisk wind whipped about the tails of my jacket. I inhaled the crisp Arctic air. I was surprised it wasn't colder at 7,000 feet, since earlier reports indicated that it was "nuking" at the top. At the 17,000-foot base camp, the temperature was forty below zero with a seventy-mile-per-hour wind.

I ducked under the wing and waved to the camera. A reporter approached me with microphone in hand. Burying my apprehension, I slipped into what had become, over the last few weeks, my public persona. Curious onlookers watched as the reporter tossed the usual questions, and I replied with the expected answers. My confidence grew when he asked, "And what do you hope to accomplish with this climb, beyond, of course, setting a new high point record?"

Squaring my shoulders, I smiled toward the camera. "More than anything else, I want to send a message to people everywhere that life's challenges do not need to stop us from reaching goals and breaking down barriers. Through personal determination and faith that God will supply the power, humans can overcome any barrier."

But my words were more confident than my feelings. I was face to face with the biggest barrier on the continent.

After the trip to the emergency room, I rested all that day and half of the next. We drove to my Uncle Bill's home outside of Boston.

This was the same uncle who had been with me during the amputation. He was once asked to become ambassador to Norway. Now he taught history at Emerson University. Even in his eighties, this very proper Bostonian gentleman exercised a sharp mind. His son-in-law was visiting from England.

We talked about my climbing experiences and about his recent illness. A month or two before my visit, he'd suffered a heart attack and stroke and had died once on the table. While I wanted to encourage him, I realized that there was a fine line between stretching oneself and causing more damage by overdoing. I remembered the lessons I learned the hard way after my injury when I accidentally pulled out stitches and IV needles.

Early on Sunday morning, we once again hit the road. Eagerly I anticipated the easy climbs along the East Coast and in the South. I'd have plenty of time to heal. The next major climb would not be until Colorado.

We headed for Rhode Island's high point, Jerimoth Hill— 812 feet. At the Rhode Island state line, we took the Hartford Pike. We'd been warned by other high pointers about Jerimoth Hill and the man who lived at the mouth of the dirt road that led to the high point. While Jerimoth Hill is owned by Brown University, the dirt road that leads to the high point runs along the edge of a property owner's home. For some reason, whenever the man spots a high pointer, he screams at them and threatens to call the police. It's been rumored that he's taken shots at them as well.

We located the big red farmhouse where the man lived and parked our truck on the other side of a nearby radio tower, 200 yards beyond the man's property. He'd parked a big tan van across the entrance to the dirt road to keep people from hiking on the road.

When we got out of the vehicle, we heard organ music coming from the man's residence. *It's Sunday morning,* I reasoned. *The man is probably getting ready to leave for church. He'll probably be in a friendlier mood.* Being a trained psychotherapist and a self-appointed guardian of the reputation of all high pointers everywhere, I grabbed the camera from the seat and announced, "I'm going to knock on the door and get his permission."

"Why?" Whit looked at me in astonishment. "We're not going to trespass on his land. Why should we bother to ask?"

"Because it's the respectful thing to do." Music poured from the open door as I strode up to the walkway. Less confident in my talents at problem solving, Whit lingered beside the road. I paused at the doorstep and raised my hand to knock, when I thought, *Whoa! Wait a minute! What makes you think the man will be nice to you? Lots of other people have tried to be polite and respectful to this guy, and he's responded with threats and possibly, bullets. I'm getting out of here!*

Instantly, I whipped about and ran as fast as I could down the walkway. "Come on," I whispered as I dashed past the startled Whit; "let's go! Let's go!"

Whit didn't need a second invitation. We charged across the highway, around the parked van the man was using to block the trail, and up the dirt road. We didn't stop running until we reached the rock cairn that represented the high point. I tossed the camera to Whit, then doubled over to catch my breath. "Hurry! Take the picture!"

I straightened, pasted a publicity smile on my face, and froze.

"Got it!" Whit shouted. "Here!"

He handed me the camera. We switched places and repeated the process. "Got it!" I stuffed the camera in my waist pack. "Come on. Let's get out of here."

We ran down the dirt road to the parked van. As I dashed across the highway to our vehicle, the man came out of his garage. Whit and I ran full speed toward our truck.

Apparently, he hadn't seen us yet, for he strode across the highway and hopped into his van. That's when he first spied us, obvious hikers, our truck bed piled high with hiking gear.

By the glare on his face, we could tell he intended to prevent us from making the climb. I chuckled out loud. "We should stay here a while and make him late."

Whit laughed. "Yeah, let the guy think we haven't done the climb yet."

"Naw, we have mountains to climb, man." I started the engine. "We're out of here."

"Can't you hear that guy mumbling under his breath as he goes in to church. 'Boy, I really showed those guys! That'll teach those confounded high pointers, coming around and bothering me!' " Whit's faked heavy New England accent made me laugh all the more.

We pulled up to a tollbooth along the Massachusetts Turnpike. Our destination: Massachusetts' 3,491- foot high point, Mt. Greylock. On this occasion, we were joined by a reporter and photographer for the climb. Talk about your on-the-site interviews! At the summit, we climbed the ninety-foot granite tower, a war memorial built in 1933. We took a few pictures of the villages in the surrounding valley, then wandered through the Bascomb Lodge cafeteria and gift shop.

From there, we dropped down below the Massachusetts-Connecticut border to 2,380-foot Mount Frissell. It seemed strange to stop three-quarters of the way to the top and have it count as the high point. The mountain is shared by the two states, and the actual peak lies across the state line into Massachusetts. Since we had already done the Massachusetts high point, we didn't have to go any higher.

"Three mountains in one day! We're doing great!" I handed the camera back to Whit. "Come on, let's head back for the truck."

On the way down the trail, I met some elderly climbers who recognized me from photos they had seen in a magazine. Again, I shared my message of overcoming challenges through God's grace and one's own determination. They discussed age as their challenge.

The relaxing drive between the high points took us past some beautiful countryside. And now was the time to relax—before we headed west.

Whit and I passed time by talking and listening to the radio.

Usually, one drove while the other slept. We had no time to waste if we were going to break the record. Always looming in the back of my mind were the western states—and the ever present concern of Mt. McKinley.

It was late by the time we pulled into Wilmington, Delaware. We faced real danger at Delaware's high point.

Other than running over a center median while turning, we found Ebright Road without any trouble. The Ebright Azimuth—high point of 442 feet—is, literally, a bump in the road, as Whit called it.

We risked our lives in traffic to pose for photographs in the middle of the busy city street. It was the closest I'd come yet to being killed!

After a night's sleep in Pennsylvania, we ate a big breakfast in a small Mennonite restaurant, then drove west. We passed neat Amish farms where farmers till their land with hand plows; their wives, dressed in black and wearing black cotton bonnets, hang their freshly washed laundry on clotheslines in the backyards. We drove past families seated in coaches painted black, driving their matching sorrels to town; and blue-and-black-clad children, swinging lunch boxes on their way to school. It was like stepping back a century or more in time.

We drove to the top of the 3,213-foot Mt. Davis, then hiked to the large boulder, a few yards west of the observation tower, to take our pictures while standing on the official high point.

As I relaxed, I began to realize how much the stress had been getting to me. As we drove to Maryland and the next high point, Backbone Mountain—3,360 feet—I realized that I had more confidence and less fear. Now I was enjoying the process.

Whit and I chose to take to take different routes to the summit. I reached the top several minutes before him. When I saw him coming, I hid behind a large tree. As he passed, I jumped out and yelled. He had no clue that I was there, so I scared him big time. I rolled on the ground, laughing.

"I'll get you big time for that one, Huston!" His vow set me cackling again.

"In what lifetime?" I choked.

We hiked back down the hill to the truck and headed west and south toward West Virginia.

Most of the 4,863-foot climb up Spruce Knob was done in the truck. We drove from Maryland across a portion of Virginia to the Monongahela National Forest and Spruce Knob Recreation Area. Since we'd been doing so much riding, both of us wanted to hike a few of the summit trails. Whit took one trail while I took another.

I hiked out through a clearing of scrub blueberry bushes and stunted mountain ash to a rock overlooking a valley. Perched upon the rock, I thought of where we'd been and where we still had to go. In my mind, I planned the rest of the route. I listed off the problems that needed solving before we returned to the west to climb Gannet, Hood, and Rainier. And McKinley.

First, we needed a McKinley guide. My first choice was Adrian, the currect record holder. Then we would need additional support. Mike, a military man who was an experienced climber, came highly recommended by other climbers. But he could only join us if we had a letter from a high-ranking senator or congressman, requesting a three-week leave. Without that, we would have to find someone else. I didn't want to do that.

Chuck, an engineer whom we met climbing, had volunteered to contact his friend, Congressman Lewis, in Washington. "Anything I can do for you, let me know."

Maybe it's time for Lisa to contact Chuck, I thought. *Oh, well, there's not much I can do from here.* With a guarded eye on the thunderstorm approaching from the west, I replaced the worrisome thoughts with more immediate concerns.

Our next high points rolled by like a Charles Kuralt travelogue: Virginia's Mount Rogers—5,729 feet; Kentucky's Black Mountain—4,145 feet; and Tennessee's Clingman's Dome—6,643 feet. We ran out of gas on our way to North Carolina's Mount Mitchell—6,684 feet. Then it was on to Sassafras Mountain—3,560 feet—in South Carolina; and Sumpter National Forest's Brasstown Bald—4,784 feet—in Georgia.

The visitor's center on Brasstown Bald, including the restrooms, had closed for the day by the time we arrived. We'd been traveling nonstop to check off four high points in one day. The place was deserted. Unable to wait until we got back down the mountain to use the restroom facility, I ambled over near what appeared to be an abandoned log cabin and satisfied my problem.

At that moment, a woman opened the front door of the cabin and walked out. Seeing what I was doing, she ducked back inside her home. Unwittingly, I'd chosen to use her front yard as a restroom facility.

Feeling the need to explain myself, I knocked on her door. When she answered, I explained that we were high pointers and we couldn't find the benchmark.

"Sure, I'll show you where it is." She led the way to a locked gate that led to a stairwell. "It's over there. If you didn't know where to look, you'd never find it."

"How are we going to stand on it to have our pictures taken?" Whit asked, eyeing the benchmark.

"I think I know a way." I stretched my leg through the iron bars and touched it with my foot. "There! Take the picture."

We talked with the woman for some time. She told us how she'd come to live on Brasstown Bald. "After my husband died and my kids were grown, I needed to find a new life for myself. Doing volunteer work at different national parks allows me to travel as well as build a new life for myself."

She talked about the challenge of getting beyond the death of one's spouse. "We were married for so many years. I had to fight depression every day that first year after he died." She understood my message completely.

During the next few days, we checked off the high point at Mississippi's Woodall Mountain—806 feet. At Florida's unnamed high point—America's lowest high point of 345 feet—I was tempted to dress in my snow clothing and gear for the picture. But it was just too hot.

I loved the view from Alabama's 2,407-foot Cheaha Mountain, the place where the Creek Indian Wars took place in 1813, but I hated the humidity. I met a black family there who were moving to a new location. The children expressed their fears about making friends and attending a new school. We talked about our faith in God and how He makes all the difference.

We slept on top of the mountain that night. Fast-moving clouds rolled overhead, occasionally giving us glimpses of the moon. The next morning we hiked back to the truck and headed north to Taum Sauk Mountain in Missouri, then back south to the Ozark National Forest and Signal Hill on top of Magazine Mountain—2,753 feet.

We spent the night at Jack Longacker's home in Mountain Home, Arkansas. Jack, a lively, talkative man, is the president of the High Pointers Club of America. He also writes the high pointers' newsletter and keeps the statistics on the climbs.

After a meal of genuine southern cuisine—beans and corn bread, we shared our clippings and photos with him, and he showed us mementos from the entire history of high pointing.

In 118-degree heat, we drove to Driskill Mountain—535 feet—in Louisiana. We had no air conditioning in the truck. We climbed at night to avoid the heat. At one point we couldn't stand the heat any longer, so we pulled off by a lake and jumped in for a few hours, until we cooled off.

Clear on the other side of Texas was the Guadeloupe Mountains National Park, where Geronimo, the chief of the Apaches, held out against the U.S. Cavalry. The sun had set by the time we headed up the 4.4-mile Guadeloupe Peak Trail to the 8,749-foot summit of Guadeloupe Peak.

"Perfect," I said. "We'll hike now while it's cooler."

It was cooler—only ninety degrees.

We slept on top in the cool air, only a few feet away from the edge of a 150-foot cliff. We had to put rocks around our sleeping bags so we wouldn't roll off in our sleep.

We woke up early and waited for the sun to rise. As soon as it cleared the horizon, we began racing down the trail. Within a very few minutes, the temperature was climbing once again. We hurried the opposite way—down. Already, it felt like we were walking in an oven. As we passed hikers on their way to the top, I hoped they had lots of water for the climb.

We had a date with another high point, a special one this time—in my home state.

CHAPTER ELEVEN

The Real Mountains Begin

Kahiltna Glacier

On our way to the ranger's station to check in, we passed numerous clusters of tents scattered across the field of snow. Each was surrounded by a wall carved out of snow; snow, the ruling force on the mountain.

Snow is the mountaineer's friend and the mountaineer's foe. Climbers walk on it, sleep on it, slide on it, and cook with it. They melt it to ward off dehydration. They use it to insulate themselves against the wind, extreme temperature drops, and unexpected mountain storms. They have to protect themselves against the snow blindness it causes, and from the sun rays that it intensifies.

Looking down at the well-scarred snow crunching beneath my boots, I marveled at how bright everything was. Though the sun had gone down, I could have read a book by the amount of light still available!

While Adrian and Whit unloaded our gear, Mike and I located the park ranger. She introduced herself as Annie.

A dental hygienist from New England, Annie spent her summers working as a park ranger for the National Park Service. She directed us to a convenient campsite.

"Would you believe the number of people here at base camp!" I whispered to Mike. "I thought we were going into the wilds of Alaska. Are they all here to climb McKinley?"

"Yes." The ranger overheard me. "Don't be fooled by these mild temperatures," she warned. "The weather station in Anchorage says they may drop tonight. There's a low-pressure system moving in. But it should be gone by Monday."

A dusting of snow fell on us as we pitched our tents and set up camp. By the time the cocoa was hot, I could feel the mountain's low temperatures in my bones. I cozied the mug between my stiffening hands and sipped the hot liquid. Since we'd arrived at the 7,000-foot base camp, I'd been incredibly thirsty. I didn't need to be reminded that, at this altitude, dehydration would be my constant enemy.

After supper I got acquainted with the climbers camping next to us. We sat around their camp stove, swapping climbing experiences. I shared with them my goal to break the world's high point record set by Adrian.

When they asked how I got interested in mountaineering, I told then about the 50 Peaks Project. "They wanted to show people that challenges need not stop anyone from accomplishing their goals."

One of the climbers whistled through his teeth. "Good luck, man. That's treacherous terrain up there, even for a two-legged man."

I grimaced. "So I hear."

A new surge of energy infused us as we drove north toward my home state, Oklahoma, and the high point, Black Mesa—4,973 feet. One of the largest mesas in the world, Black Mesa's eighty acres spill over into Colorado and New Mexico. Located on the far western end of Oklahoma's panhandle, and once known as No Man's Land, the area harbored bandits and outlaws in the mid-1800s.

During our climb up Black Mesa the next day, we met a third- and fourth-grade school group from Felt. I gave them an impromptu talk at the summit. "Don't look at people with disabilities like they can't do anything—they just have a different and difficult kind of challenge to overcome."

We signed autographs and posed for photographs with the kids on the granite summit marker. The group invited me to hike back down with them. On the way down, right in front of me, one of their teachers took a sudden fall. "Let's all stay back and keep calm," I told the kids as I carefully lifted a rock off her leg. Whit and the other teacher carried her down the steep hill while I led the kids along behind.

"It's a good thing we were here," I said to Whit as we drove into Kenton to register our climb at the Kenton Mercantile. From there, I called the park rangers for information on the conditions of the western states' trails. They reported that the snow had been melting rapidly and the trails looked great.

Lightning flashed and thunder roared from the heavy cloud bank to the west of us as we drove north toward Kansas's 4,039-foot Mount Sunflower on the Colorado-Kansas border. We were occasionally pounded by hail and heavy rain, but we always kept an eye out for a tornado.

The storm had cleared by the time we drove to the summit and posed for pictures beside the unique, six-foot-high sun-flower made of railroad spikes that marks this high point. Nearby, another hand-printed marker read, "On this site in 1897, nothing happened."

Exhilaration coursed through me as I drove north from Mount Sunflower to the town of Kangarado, Kansas. I tapped out the rhythm to a jazz number on the radio. I felt good, really good. We'd checked off the thirty-eighth state in less than thirty days. Colorado's Mount Elbert—14,433 feet— would be the thirty-ninth. The best part—we were weeks ahead of the record. "I think we just might make it!"

"Huh? What?" Whit looked over at me in surprise.

"We're gonna do it! With God's help, we're gonna break the high point record."

We hiked up Mount Elbert's eleven-mile primary route in the early morning because summer afternoons on the moun-tain often bring showers and thunderstorms. We didn't want to get caught on one of the mountain's exposed ridges in a freezing rain or a snow storm—or an electrical storm. Re-cently, a climber had been struck by lightning and killed on Mt. Elbert.

I felt the elevation as I climbed the last thousand feet. I was a little short of breath, but otherwise I felt strong. On the way down the 14,433-foot mountain, I found traces of mountain sheep. I'd hoped to spot at least one while on the mountain, but it wasn't to be that day.

I accelerated my pace, swinging my arms as I walked, giving my praises to God. My leg and my toe had healed sufficiently so as not to pain me with each step. I felt good, really good.

Back at the truck, I studied the road map, trying to decide which was the best route to New Mexico's 13,161-foot Wheeler Peak. That night, I thought I could lick the world. Or at least, New Mexico's Wheeler Peak.

Driving the winding roads south to the Wheeler Peak Wilderness area of Carson National Forest took most of the next day. We eased the truck into the parking area designated especially for hikers in the Taos Ski Valley and slept. The next morning I climbed out of the vehicle and stretched. I was definitely ready to hit the trail. We hiked the Blue Lake trail to the three-foot-high stone and mortar monument atop the peak's high point, took our photos, then headed back down a shorter but steeper route. We arrived back at our truck, tired and thirsty.

We drove to Taos, where I called Lisa for an update on the media arrangements she was making for Arizona's high point.

"We got him!" she shared excitedly. "Congressman Lewis wrote the letter arranging for Mike's military leave. He can join you in Wyoming!"

I leapt for joy. With Mike along on McKinley, we had a real shot at the record.

From Taos, we headed south to Sante Fe, then west on I-40 across New Mexico and Arizona to Flagstaff. After a short pit stop, we drove the ten miles north of Flagstaff to Humphreys Peak, the main peak of the four San Francisco Peaks in the Kachina Peaks Wilderness Area of Coconino National Forest. Like Alaska's Denali, the 12,633-foot mountain is sacred to nearby Native American tribes.

We had climbed Humphreys Peak once before for practice. One of our early climbs, it was my first real experience with high altitudes and snow. I quickly discovered that I didn't have the right equipment for snow climbing. Since we didn't have snowshoes or crampons, both my good leg and my prosthesis kept post-holing. When that happened, I punched through the snow and sank down deep.

On that trip I wondered with each step if I would sink into the snow an inch or up to my waist. Broken tree limbs buried under the snow sometimes threw me off balance, face down in the snow. I prayed I would summit and get down the mountain without breaking my new leg.

When it grew dark, we had a hard time deciding which of the many trails led to the top. *Great,* I thought, *next we'll be lost on this mountain all night!*

We kept climbing as a ferocious wind buffeted us about, freezing our fingers. On top, we signed the register and started back down. In spite of my discomfort, I felt good, really good. I could barely contain my exhilaration.

I'd climbed my first real mountain!

But the climb should be easier this time. It was later in the year and much warmer. The snow was gone. At 5:30 the next morning, Sarah Jane, a reporter from a local paper, met me in the field below the mountain. She shot a few photos before I asked her if she'd like to climb the mountain.

"Me? No way! I could never climb Humphreys."

I smiled. "Well, you know, part of my purpose for climbing all fifty high points is to encourage others to overcome their limitations. Maybe I can help you too."

She shook her head in disbelief. "I don't know." I spotted a glimmer of desire in her eyes.

"Aw, come on," Whit urged. "We'll help you."

She took a deep breath. "OK, I'll give it a try."

We maintained a constant pace up the mountain. At one point, my artificial leg slid between two rocks, and I fell hard. But I'd come to realize that spills are a part of hiking.

With a little help and lots of encouragement, Sarah Jane made it to the top and back down again. At the summit, we wrote our names in the register.

With thoughts of success hovering in our heads, we took our time on the way back down to the trail head.

"I did it! I did it! Yes!" Sarah Jane shouted for all to hear.

We parted; she headed south and we, north to Salt lake City. The 500-mile ride took us past ruggedly beautiful scenery. *One day,* I promised myself, *I'll return and hike the back trails of Zion National Park, and I'll climb atop Bryce Canyon National Park's red sandstone arches or towering spires. Some day . . .*

Kirsten, a friend of Sarah Jane's and a reporter with a local newspaper, met us on the steps to the capitol building, where she interviewed me. Rick Porter, from the 50 Peaks Project, also met us there. He wanted to videotape our climb up Utah's King's Peak.

We spent a relaxing evening touring Salt Lake City with friends, then drove to Rick's home and met his wife, Natalie, and their children. I called Lisa to discuss Rick's proposal, then talked with Whit. We agreed to pay Rick to tape the climb.

We piled into the truck and drove east out of Salt Lake City to Wyoming, doubling back to the High Uintas Wilderness area of the Wasatch and Ashley National Forests. The guidebook said that hikers usually take two to five days to make the strenuous 28.8-mile hike to the top of 13,528-foot Kings Peak.

We camped at Henry's Fork Basin campground and started the climb. We wanted to get as far as we could on our first day out. Whit went on ahead, and I set a slower pace to protect my stump from the extreme abuse it takes on the more difficult mountains. I came to a stream and sat down on a rock to rest. Just then, a troop of Boy Scouts emerged from the woods and started to cross the stream.

One of the boys turned and looked at me curiously; then he noticed my artificial leg. "Hey, you're the guy with one leg who's climbing all the mountains! I saw your picture in the paper last night!"

I grinned. "That's right. I'm the guy." Lisa's publicity work was paying off. We were recognized almost everywhere we went.

A second Scout walked closer to where I sat. "Everybody's talking about you."

"Oh?"

"Yeah, you're some kind of hero."

The other boys gathered around the rock. Questions flew for the next hour. One boy asked, "Were you ever a Boy Scout?"

"I sure was, an Eagle Scout too. I loved Scouting. We had great times going camping in the wilderness. Our troop leaders taught us about safe hiking practice, about emergency techniques, as well as teaching us important lessons in character building and honesty."

We joked around for a while longer; then I resumed my climb up to 11,888-foot Gunsight Pass, a mountain pass shaped like the *V* on the gun sight of a rifle. I caught up with Whit there, and we stopped at the top of the pass to wait for Rick to catch up with us.

"Since you have to move slower, maybe you should go on while I wait for him," Whit suggested. "You can find us a good camping spot."

"Good idea." At the foot of the hill, I checked the map to discover which was the right trail. The shorter trail went through marshy glacier terrain covered with underbrush. The longer trail was higher and dryer. I chose the high road. At Anderson Pass, I looked back and saw Whit and Rick on the trail behind me. I hiked back down to meet them. When I reached Whit, Rick was nowhere in sight.

"Where's Rick?"

Whit cast me a wry grin. "He's a half mile back. He says he's blown out, says he won't go another step."

I glanced around us. Small clumps of bushes dotted the reasonably flat surrounding area. "We could camp here for the night."

"Good idea. I'll go back and get Rick." Whit hiked back to where he had left Rick and brought him to our chosen campsite.

We ate our dehydrated food as the sun set. With our sleeping bags laid out on the ground, we watched as a canopy of stars filled the clear night sky. I took out a book on astronomy I'd purchased along the way and tried to identify the constellations. Before we went to sleep, we talked about the next day's climb. We would summit, then hike straight back to the trail head.

After breakfast, Rick set out ahead of me so he could get some good sequences of me climbing the last few yards to the top of the mountain. The trail started out mellow, slowly gaining altitude. Rick bounced about, taking video footage of me as I hopped over the rocks above the timberline. Climbing up the ridge to King's Peak, the rocks became boulders. He taped me signing the register at the summit and gazing thoughtfully out over the beautiful valley and the towering peaks and plateaus surrounding us.

I strolled over to the marker and read aloud the insignia. "In honor of Clarence King (1848-1901), an American geologist who . . ." I read aloud the words on the plaque on the summit of King's Peak in Utah. Hearing a shuffle behind me, I turned, expecting to see Whit. "Hey, Whit. Did you know—"

"Hi." A honey-blond woman in her twenties with a great smile on her face and a black lab by her side, paused a few feet away from me.

"Hi, yourself." I couldn't help but smile in return.

CHAPTER TWELVE

Froze-to-Death Plateau

Kahiltna Glacier

As the raucous banter flew back and forth between the seasoned mountaineers, my own thoughts flew ahead to the next day's adventure. Later that night, I climbed into my sleeping bag, rolled over onto my side, and whispered into my recorder. "I choke up whenever I think about what God is doing for me. Why me? So many people are praying for me. I feel overwhelmed, yet scared." I clicked the button on the recorder and set it beside my head.

I stared at the semidark dome of nylon arching over my head and thought about my purpose for climbing the mountain. I thought about all the people who would hear my story and be inspired to climb their own "mountains," whatever those mountains might be. Then I remembered the horror stories of avalanches, rock slides, whiteouts, and crevasses. Like a kid making a birthday wish, I squeezed my eyes shut. "God, I need You more than ever. Help me to be strong and remain close to You."

We awakened to blue skies and brilliant sunlight. After a breakfast of rehydrated oatmeal, hot chocolate, and hot cider, the four of us roped up and walked six miles up the glacier. Sunlight sparkled off the ice falls and crevasses, creating a kaleidoscope of whites and deep blues surrounding the outcroppings of rocks.

Every direction we looked, we saw lofty mountains. However, beyond the beauty of the glacier, beyond the host of lesser peaks, one could feel the presence of The Mountain, always The Mountain.

"It's so high!" I craned my neck to study its splendor. Rising almost three miles above us, The Mountain took my breath away. All the superlatives I knew paled in the shadow of the Great One. I felt like a Lilliputian stepping into Gulliver's Land of Giants. "It's awesome!"

The conversations on the glacier were always spoken in hushed tones, like in a majestic cathedral. Being a naive beginner, I talked with other climbers, eager like me to begin their ascent. I spoke with the sunburned, beat-up climbers coming down off the mountain, almost too exhausted to reply. "It's rough up there," one admitted as he trudged past me.

"Rough up there." I thought about his words as we trudged back to our campsite. *How rough is rough?* I wondered.

It hadn't seemed so rough back in Utah. The blond woman smiled again.

"You're the guy in the news who's out to break the record for climbing the fifty peaks, aren't you?"

"Guess so." I extended my hand. "I'm Todd Huston."

"My name's Barbara." She glanced down at her half–black Lab/half-mutt dog. "And this is Kona."

"Hi, Kona." I patted the animal's head. He rewarded me with a lick. "Are you a park ranger or something?"

She laughed. "No, why do you ask?"

"You look like you spend a lot of time outdoors. You're in great shape."

She tipped her head to one side and laughed. "I do spend a fair amount of time outside. I'm a mountain guide at Telluride."

"I knew it." I snapped my fingers. "What do you do when you're not guiding groups up mountains?"

"Well . . ." She hesitated. "I do a little skiing."

I eyed her curiously. "Why do I get the feeling that there's more to this story than you're telling?"

"OK, I'm a member of the United States 1993 Women's Extreme Ski Team."

"Really? So what are you doing up here on King's Peak?" I found out later that she was also the '93 Extreme Ski Champion.

She waved her hand out over the rock ledge. "The same thing you are—climbing mountains."

I introduced her to Whit and Rick. The four of us talked for a while about the mountains we had climbed and the ones we looked forward to climbing.

"I go from here to Gannett Peak in Wyoming." Barbara shifted her weight from one foot to the other. Kona sprawled out at her feet for a nap. "I hear it's a strenuous climb."

"That's where we're heading," I said. "How many are in your climbing team?"

"Just me."

"Ooh." I grimaced. "You might want other climbers with you on that one. It's more of a technical climb—ropes, crampons, ice axes, and all. Hey, why don't you hike with us?"

"Really? You or your partners wouldn't mind?"

Whit's eyes widened. "No way would I mind."

I laughed. "Naw. A new face would be welcome, I'm sure."

We took the steep route on the west side of Anderson Pass back down the mountain. Rick and Whit went ahead in order to pack our gear for the next climb while Barbara, Kona, and I took our time, especially over the loose-rock area. She told me that she was troubled about her relationship with her boyfriend. "Maybe it's because my dad died last year and I feel so empty without him. I don't know." She paused. "You're a psychoanalyst. You tell me."

I smiled. "It sounds like you're doing enough psychoanalyzing for both of us."

"I just wish I could have spent more time with him."

"I think I can understand a little bit of what you're saying. My wife left me last year. It seems she only married me to get her green card."

"Oh, I'm sorry. Then you do understand loneliness. So many people say they understand how you feel, when they really don't."

"Yeah." I nodded in agreement. "They're only trying to help. Sometimes they don't know what else to say."

"I suppose."

We got to where we were supposed to meet Whit and Rick along the trail, but they were nowhere in sight. Exhausted, I found a rock beside a stream and sat down. My legs ached. This had been the longest hike since Mt. Marcy in New York State.

Barbara tossed her backpack on the ground. "Hey, are you hungry?"

"Hungry? Are you kidding?" My stomach growled as I spoke.

"Well, then you rest your leg, and I'll cook us a supper." She pulled a camp stove out of her pack and went to work. Before long, Kona was eating his supper while we talked and ate ours.

A half-hour after twilight, Whit and Rick arrived. They had taken a different trail, which turned out to be longer. By the time we hit the trail once more, we needed to use our head lamps.

Back at the parking lot, Barbara and Kona headed for her Mazda pickup and makeshift camper while Whit, Rick, and I threw our sleeping bags on the ground. My aching legs didn't keep me awake that night.

The next day I rode with Barbara to Jackson Hole and learned more about her. She got into skiing when she was twenty-one, had been featured on the front of *Ski* magazine, and did modeling in addition to her championship skiing. "I do skiing commercials for Visa Card too," she added.

"Magazine or television?"

"TV. Maybe you've seen the Visa ad where the blonde jumps out of a helicopter, lands, and skis down the mountain."

"Yeah! That's you?"

She shrugged and laughed. "Some of us will do anything for money."

I asked to see her portfolio and her publicity scrapbook.

"You're really interested, aren't you?" She sounded surprised. "You're not asking just to be polite."

"Of course I'm interested."

We hit Jackson Hole, Wyoming, late that afternoon. Whit and Rick pulled in behind us. I had arranged to meet Mike in Jackson Hole.

"There he is." I pointed toward the parking lot up the street. Barbara parked her truck, and I climbed out. "Mike," I called and waved, "over here."

It was great to see him again. I introduced him to Barbara and Kona. Mike and Barbara hit it off right away. They became great friends.

"Congressman Lewis came through," he said, "at least for a portion of the climbs. I won't be able to do Mt. Hood with you though, huh?"

I shrugged. "I guess."

"What are you going to do? You can't hike that one without a guide."

"I don't know, except pray about it." I heaved a deep sigh. I had been thinking about this dilemma ever since I learned that the while the U.S. Army granted Mike a leave, it was to be much shorter than we had hoped.

"God knows our need. He's come through for me so far. Why should He quit now?"

Mike smiled. I wasn't sure he understood, but he had gotten used to my talking about God in a personal way. He glanced down at his watch. "If we're going to get our gear for tomorrow's hike, we'd better hit the mountaineering store."

We bought the necessary food and supplies, then headed for a pizza parlor. While the gang ate pizza, I placed a call to Hawaii. Lisa had arranged for me to check in with a DJ on a radio station where I would do interviews about the day's climb, in anticipation for the last high point, Mauna Kea on the Big Island.

With the phone call out of the way, we dropped Barbara's truck off at her boyfriend's house and headed toward Gannett Peak. Gannett Peak—13,804 feet high—sits on the border of the Bridger Wilderness and the Fitzpatrick Wilderness. To scale it, one must hike 20.2 miles to the top, then back down again.

We pitched our tents in an open field to avoid being pestered by bugs.

A ranger stopped by. "Watch out for a skier who we're presuming died in an avalanche a few months ago on Dinwittie Pass. We've found one ski and his poles so far."

Before dawn the next morning, we set out on the trail, our head lamps lighting the way. It wasn't long before the early-morning light revealed the incredible beauty around us. A variety of wildflowers dotted the fields and forest pathways. Five miles up the trail I paused at Photographer's Point to admire the gorgeous view.

There I met a family from Costa Rica. While the parents looked on, I told their twelve-year-old son and their eight-year-old daughter how important it was to have faith in God. When I finished, the mother said, "Don't we always tell you that?"

I met a botanist and his hiking partner, an engineer. The botanist told me about the wildflowers indigenous to the Rocky Mountains. "Bluebonnets, asters, elephant ears. You're here at the most perfect time to appreciate the flowers."

I gazed about me. "It's like walking on a multicolored cloud."

From the top of Dinwittie Pass, I caught my first glimpse of Gannett Peak. *Hm,* I thought, *it doesn't look that far away.*

We pushed on to get across some narrow snow bridges over crevasses while it was still early and the snow was firm like steel. Once the sun hit it, that steel-like snow could turn to gelatin.

At the top of Glacier Gooseneck Pinnacle, Whit pointed toward one of the many high peaks spread out before us. "There's the summit over there."

I looked at the peak at which he was pointing, then at the one just to its left. Both peaks looked the same to me. "Are you sure?"

Mike came up behind us. "Yeah, that's the one—the one to the right."

I shook my head. "The one on the left seems higher to me."

"Well," Mike reasoned, "we'll be able to tell when we get a little closer." Mike sped on ahead while we hiked on down the glacier where three experienced rock climbers caught up with us.

"Can you tell us which of those two is Gannett Peak?" I asked.

"That one," the oldest man answered, pointing toward the peak on the left.

About then, Mike called back to us. "It's the one on the left. I can tell by the trail." We had to laugh.

Stepping up the pace, we soon came to a bergstrom, an area where the snow is pulling away from the mountain. Soon, it would be a crevasse. "Time to rope up," Mike said.

I roped up with Barbara. (Kona had stayed at the campsite during our summit climb. Black Labs don't come with natural crampons on their feet.) Together, we inched our way up the snow bowl, constantly aware of Rick's whirring video camera. The winds really whipped over us. As long as I climbed, I was sweating. When I stopped, I got chilly. After a walk up a steep snowfield full of snow cups, we reached the top.

After a rest and a nice visit with some other climbers, we started down. As was often the case, going down was more difficult than climbing for me. Mike and I roped up for the trip over the bergstrom. When my Flex-foot post-holed, I knew I was in trouble.

But I didn't know how much trouble until I poked my ski pole into the snow where my foot had gone down. It punched straight through into a crevasse forty to one hundred feet deep.

My mouth dropped open, and for a second or so I just stared down the hole next to where I stood. Then my senses returned and I leapt back, doubly thankful that we'd taken time to rope up.

From that point, we walked along the edge of the bergstrom instead of on the glacier itself. Beneath our feet, we could see water flowing under the ice cap. When we finally stepped on solid rock, I whispered a heartfelt prayer of gratitude.

We kept a steady pace throughout the rest of the climb despite the swelling in my stump and the soreness in my good leg. I hurried into my tent when we reached camp, took off my leg, drank some water, climbed into my bag, and slept.

After a night's rest, we headed for the base camp and our

vehicles. We stayed in Jackson Hole for an extra day so I could rest and do some business—and to treat ourselves to hot showers and a nice meal out.

We said goodbye to Barbara and Kona the next morning and headed north to Montana. In Custer National Forest stood Granite Peak. If any mountain in the lower forty-eight could keep us from making all fifty climbs, this one was it.

At Granite Peak, we hiked from the trail head to a lake, then up the side of the mountain toward Froze-to-Death Plateau. There the trail got steeper and rockier as it switchbacked up the mountain.

The U.S. Forest Service warns people about the plateau: "A snowstorm can occur any month of the year." Fortunantly for us, the weather at the moment was clear and comfortable.

After the plateau, we encountered a field of rocks piled on top of one another. It was hard hopping from rock to rock, constantly guarding against the possibility of slipping or falling.

We climbed for nine hours that first day. Since a major rock climb still loomed ahead of us, I suggested we take a day off so I could rest. Mike spent the day training Whit and Rick in technical climbing. They learned how to balay rope across rocks.

By four the next morning, we were hiking down the side of Tempest Mountain. Next we climbed up the ridge that connected it with Granite Peak. We roped up when we reached the boulder area. After testing the slings, we used them and the webbing left by guide groups to climb the boulders.

Occasionally, as I balayed across a sheer drop, I'd glance down at the thousand feet of air below me and congratulate myself on not panicking. Several times, we heard a minor rock slide in the distance. Of course, no rock slide is minor if a rock hits you in the head.

We scaled the huge rock walls to the Crux, the hardest part of the ascent. Next was the Key Hole, two rocks perpendicular to the mountain with another slab on top. Fifty to a hundred feet beyond the Key Hole was the summit.

"Yahoo!" I shouted as I stamped my boot on the bench mark. "We made it!"

I was the first to rappel down the rock on the return trip. I let myself down on a ledge by traversing twenty or thirty feet to the right, then undid the rope and set it for Whit.

I loved this climb. For once, depending on my upper body strength, I was faster than the able-bodied climbers.

Suddenly, above me, Whit slipped. Instinctively, I pulled the rope tight. Whit got another hold and soon joined me. The others followed without incident.

At the Crux, we rappelled down another thousand feet onto a ledge eighteen inches wide we were anchored in. From there Mike led the way down the ridge to a snow bridge. "Kodak moment!" he shouted halfway across. Then he snapped a picture of me at the edge of the bridge.

"Ahhh!" The shout behind us was followed by clanging and banging. I whirled to see Rick fall on his backside and begin to slide down a thousand-foot slope of snow and ice.

Rocks and snow tumbled down ahead of him. Then as suddenly as he had started sliding, his heel caught on a rock, stopping his fall.

"Don't move!" Mike shouted. He ran to the edge and surveyed the danger. Then he led Rick back to safety. Whit and I just stared at each other. *Whoa!*

Grateful and somewhat solemn, we followed the cairns back to Froze-to-Death Plateau. The sky was dark and the wind whipped fiercely around us as we started across.

Then the storm broke. Lightning bolts struck all around us. With sheer cliffs on each side, there was nowhere to run or hide. We were at the mercy of the elements. I prayed and walked as fast as I could.

Fortunantely, most of the storm hit a mountain peak to the north of us. I enjoyed the dramatic light show in spite of my concerns. At the edge of the plateau, I spotted three climbers heading up. One of them shouted, "Is that you, Todd?"

I squinted my eyes, trying to identify the man.

"It's Ron. Remember me?" The Seventh-day Adventist pastor from Oregon had met me on another mountain.

"Ron, how are things going?" I stopped to talk with him as the others went on. When I learned that Ron was planning to climb Idaho's high point a few days later, we agreed to meet there.

Once at the bottom, we packed up to head for Idaho. We stopped in Bozeman, Montana, to meet with my friend Fred, who was in town visiting friends. It was great to see Fred again—he had always been so supportive of the adventure.

Voni, the friend he was visiting, was supportive too. "God is using you, Todd. He's given you such an incredible opportunity to influence so many people's lives. He's putting you in a position to do so."

She spoke with total conviction. I had heard it from Lisa and from family members, but coming from a stranger, a newfound friend, it inspired me more than ever. Without my explaining, she saw what the climb was all about.

There had been so many times on the trail when my strength threatened to fail me, when the pain in my legs seemed so intense I thought I couldn't go on, when I wanted to step off the trail and say, "I'm finished. I've had it."

At those times, I repeated over and over to myself, "I've got to keep walking. I'm doing this for God. I've got to get down off this mountain."

We drove across Montana and Idaho to Borah Peak, where we met Dan and Mike, two reporters who found this to be a great excuse to get out of the office. We introduced ourselves, then set up camp. I discovered an older gentleman who had planned to climb the peak alone and invited him to join our team.

Ron and his buddies hadn't shown up by the time we sacked out for the night. They arrived before dawn the next morning, ready to do some serious climbing.

Starting at the trail head, Mt. Borah proved to be an extremely steep hike. That was hard enough, but then we reached a knife-edge ridge. With 1,200-foot dropoffs on both sides, we were fotunate to have great handholds.

The snow bridge to the summit was an easy walk across, but one slip would have sent a person a long way. We could see ski poles lying farther down the slope, but didn't know if the unlucky skier was down there too.

During the whole trip, I was careful to do only what was necessary to make the climb successful. I didn't want to take chances just for fun—chances that could lead to a loss of time, unnecessary exposure, or injury.

As Ron and I hiked, we talked about our faith in God and what it means to have Him actively involved in one's life.

"You know, Ron, I've got to get a book out on this project. I know God is going to use my experience to help others. A book will help me do that."

He thought for a few seconds. "I have some Christian contacts in the publishing business who may be able to help you. If you'd like, I can make a few phone calls."

"Would you? Really? That would be great." Again, I was overwhelmed by the way God worked out His will in my life. A Scripture text from Proverbs popped into my mind. "In all your ways acknowledge him, and he will make straight your paths."

Talking about ideas for the book, we hiked to the summit, registered the climb, then climbed back down the mountain. At the trail head, Ron said goodbye. "I'll make that call right away."

"Great."

Most of the mountains were now behind us. Even though we had slowed down a lot lately, breaking the record still seemed very possible.

It was time.

Time to face McKinley. The record, the success of the whole expedition, would ride my back to the top of McKinley.

All along the way, whenever I was interviewed by the press, I had said, "Mount McKinley will be a challenge. It's a big mountain. But you have to respect every climb, large or small."

Over dinner that night, fear and anxiety gripped me as we discussed the next leg of our journey—Spokane, then on to McKinley. It was like everything we'd done so far was but a warm-up for the Great One.

CHAPTER THIRTEEN

Heading to Alaska

The peaceful drive through the Idaho forests did little to still my anxieties. Quite the contrary, the mountains intensified my fears. Somewhere in the background of my thoughts I could hear a Spokane radio talk-show host arguing with an irate caller about the positive and negative effects of the Clinton health plan. Normally I would be spouting my personal opinions on the subject, but this time the issues couldn't begin to hold my attention.

Whit glanced over at me from the driver's seat, his eyes bright with excitement. He pounded the back of his right hand on the steering wheel. "Can you believe it, man? We're heading for the big one! Mount McKinley!"

I nodded. "Yeah, man—the big one!"

Everything I had heard about the killer mountain reinforced my fears. Books, pamphlets, magazine articles, and experienced climbers all warned of the genuine dangers inherent in a McKinley assault—the crevasses, the glacier, the sheer ice walls, the violent storms, plummeting temperatures, whiteouts. Leaning my head back against the headrest, I closed my eyes. A vision passed before me. A vision of walking across the snow, hearing a loud crack, then disappearing into a crevasse, frozen and lost forever—the same video had played in my mind for weeks.

Caught in a maze of my nagging self-doubt and awesome fear, I continued to brood over the potential tragedies Mount McKinley promised as we clicked off the miles. The thought that I would die on Mount McKinley refused to be stilled. I remembered the question the Israelites asked when they found themselves trapped by the approaching Egyptians. "God, did You bring us out into this wilderness to die?"

No! I shook the thought out of my mind. *My God doesn't operate that way. He's a God of love, not a god to fear. He brought me this far. He'll go the distance. But what if He wants me to turn back? What if I've misinterpreted His will all along?* Conquering McKinley meant more to me than the challenge and the victory. It was an obstacle in the way of my sharing the message God gave to me to share with others.

Todd . . . Idly, I massaged my stump to ease the residual pain from the last climb. *Be reasonable. You've tasted a little snow, some high winds, a little high altitude, and did well. You'll be fine on Mount McKinley. You'll be fine.*

Yet, as my father's red Ford pickup gobbled up the miles, my consternation intensified. For Whit, reaching the summit of McKinley was the challenge of another climb; for me, it was the reason for the entire high point project. If I could, calling upon God's power and strength, conquer the monster mountain, whose immensity I could only imagine, I could conquer whatever other challenges life threw at me. And if a one-legged amputee could scale the massive ice walls and stand victorious on the top of the North American continent, so thousands of other people that would hear my story could take hope and triumph over even the most impossible odds in their lives.

A knot formed in my throat. I swallowed hard. "OK, God, it's You and me—from the first to the last."

I settled back as the interstate signs announced the Spokane exits. The sun had dropped behind the mountains by the time Whit drove into his friends' driveway. We had arranged to leave the pickup there when we went to the airport.

While Whit visited with his friends, I called Lisa, then took a hot shower and retired for the night. Worn out from the climbs and the long drive, I quickly fell into a deep sleep.

The next afternoon I called Lisa again. We discussed the upcoming McKinley climb and how we could attract the optimum media coverage.

"You really need video footage of your climb, Todd. The TV stations I've contacted are all asking for it. And later, when you go out to speak, you'll wish you had it." As she spoke, I could imagine her tapping her number-two pencil on the desktop in my second bedroom, the base of operations for Summit America.

"I know. I promise, I'll see what I can do."

On our second day in Spokane, Whit unloaded our gear from the truck. After he sorted our jackets into one pile, our rope and snowshoes in another, and hung our sleeping bags from the porch lights, his friends' lawn looked like we were ready for a weekend Yard Sale. While repacking our gear, we did a major clothes washing.

I called Adrian Crane, the guide for the McKinley ascent. His British accent and droll wit came through the phone lines. "All's A-OK on my end," he assured me.

Adrian, the current high point record holder, had originally been connected with the 50 Peaks Project. He had been hired to guide the group up Mt. McKinley. When it dissolved, I asked him to guide the "Summit America" team.

We talked about the supplies we would need to buy in Anchorage. "Instead of joining you in the lower forty-eight, why don't I fly on an earlier flight and purchase the food—save some time, you know."

"Good idea. See you tomorrow night." I hung up the receiver and scratched off the last item on my checklist.

The next morning we boarded the plane for Seattle. Eager to be underway, Whit bounded ahead of me down the jetway. A blend of excitement and dread stirred my insides as I located my seat and prepared for takeoff. *Stay focused, Todd.* I smiled to myself. *Remember why you're doing this. Yes, you have to do the climb, but it's OK to enjoy it while you're at it, you know.*

Enjoying myself was a new thought. I had worked so long and so hard preparing for this moment, there had been little time to actually enjoy myself. I mulled over the strange concept throughout the flight.

We changed planes in Seattle. Though it was evening by the time we landed in Anchorage, the lingering sunlight made it seem hours earlier. At the airport we met up with Adrian and Mike. Mike's expertise was a godsend to the project.

From there we hired a taxi, a Subaru station wagon from Denali Overland Transportation, drove to Adrian's friends' home for supper, then headed for the REI store. Mike looked like the proverbial kid in a candy store as we purchased the necessary snow tents, additional rope, snowshoes, sleeping bags, camping gear, and extra batteries, for the McKinley climb. We also rented the plastic boots and gaiters necessary for snow climbing. I eyed the growing mound of gear.

"Is that all?" the clerk asked. I gulped and nodded.

The clerk didn't even blink when he tabulated the bill. "That will be $3,115.00, Mr. Huston, after your 20 percent discount, of course."

Though I knew that our safety depended on using the right gear, I reluctantly removed my checkbook from my jacket pocket. *"Oh, well, no turning back now, is there, Lord?"*

As we loaded the gear into the vehicle. I noted the physical contrasts between the three team members upon whom I was entrusting my life and one good limb. Outgoing and muscular, 6'2" Whit could always turn a pretty woman's head. The small, wiry Englishman with the easy smile—he also had the strength to do such a climb, and the experience. Adrian's eyes belied the serious undertones and the competitive spirit beneath his outgoing, laid-back attitude. Having grown up climbing in Scotland's difficult weather, he had an incredible sixth sense for the mountains.

Mike demonstrated a seriousness and determination that spoke of experience and confidence. His military training made him thorough when planning. His massive forearms bore witness to years of rock climbing. We called him Popeye.

As Whit slung the last package into the rear of the car, he straightened and looked around. "Hey, I'm hungry! When do we eat?"

Whit was hungry again. I laughed. *Everything's normal; all's right with the world.* After a quick bite, we headed for Talkeetna.

That night in the bunkhouse, I listened to other climbers telling about their harrowing experiences on the mountain, their mistakes, what they would do differently, what they would never do again. I heard stories of climbers who would never do anything again.

"One couple, a gung-ho army man and his girlfriend, learned the hard way a few days back," one of the climbers volunteered. "They hiked to the summit from the 14,000-foot base camp. On their way back down, on Denali Pass, the guy slipped and fell. In an attempt to stop his fall, he grabbed the woman and ended up taking her with him."

I listened intently as he continued. "They rolled more than 500 feet down the slope and lacked the strength to climb out. That's where other climbers found them. By the time the rescue team got to the scene, the woman was dead—not from the fall, but from exposure. Her macho boyfriend lived but lost some toes and fingers as well as part of his feet."

"It happens on a lot of mountains. This year on Mount Washington, in fact," one of the other climbers explained. "A real wise guy pushed himself and his fellow climber beyond their endurance. An accident happened, and he lives while the friend dies."

I shuddered at the images of death the stories projected in my mind. I recalled all the times my mother cautioned me to "learn from other people's mistakes." *How appropriate her advice is up here!*

Was I really ready for McKinley? Tomorrow I would find out—one way or the other.

CHAPTER FOURTEEN

Through Kahiltna Pass

Life at the Kahiltna Glacier was quiet but friendly.

"Hello there." A voice came from the camp on the other side of ours. "How are things?"

We turned and gestured for the two climbers to join us. The new arrivals, both men in their fifties, introduced themselves as the Peter Pan Expedition Team. "You know, after the fairy-tale character who refused to grow up? Chuck and I are following his example."

We all laughed. I learned that Peter was an emergency room physician and Chuck an engineer.

Good, I thought, *it makes me feel better having a medical doctor on the mountain should we get into trouble.* Then I remembered the tales I'd heard about finding some poor guy trapped under layers of ice for twenty years or more. *Maybe having a doctor nearby doesn't matter that much.*

We talked excitedly about the good fortune of encountering one another like we did. I smiled, for I knew that this meeting in the wilds of Alaska was not an accident or due to chance. I knew that our good fortune had come straight from God's hand.

Old Denali is wild, unpredictable, and tangled. Cliffs of rock soar thousands of feet straight into the sky. Glaciers apron her snowcapped peaks, and the roar of avalanches echoes through her valleys.

I had plenty of time that day to wax poetic about McKinley. We spent all day transporting our gear to the 8,000-foot camp.

Beyond the sores and swelling, the heat rash, and the blisters caused by the artificial limb, it takes an amputee 30 percent more energy to walk than it does a two-legged individual. Besides, one infected blister could prevent the success of the entire expedition.

So I watched the guys rope up and trudge up Ski Hill toward Kahiltna Pass to the 10,000-foot camp. Climbing atop a bare rock, I inhaled the incredible beauty surrounding me. "Oh, God," I prayed, "even in this remote area of the world, You let me know You are with me. Thank You, Father for using me in Your great plan."

I paused for a moment in the stillness, then continued. "I have no doubt but that You've given me the ability to overcome the challenges I need to face—bingo! That's it! That's the message I need to share, isn't it?"

I laughed aloud. I'd been having trouble putting into words the part about believing in one's own abilities, but now it was clear. "My mission can be summed up as, 'By having faith in God and a belief in the abilities He's given me, I can overcome any challenge.' Yes, that's it!"

A brisk wind forced me back into the tent, where I spent the rest of the day reading and sleeping. The team returned to the base camp by late afternoon.

The next morning as we loaded our packs, I pushed any negative thoughts from my mind and gave in to the thrill of the climb. We roped up—first, Mike, our guide; then Whit; me; and Adrian. It was important to place the two experienced climbers on each end. We trekked out to the main part of the glacier and headed north toward the glowering giant.

We followed the imprints in the snow. I glanced back, hoping to catch one last glimpse of the camp, but it was already swallowed up in the mist. Only a monochromatic sea of grays met my gaze.

We hiked up Ski Hill. It seemed to go on forever. And forever means something different when every breath is a struggle and every step an exercise in pain. At the 10,000-foot camp, we stopped for the night. While Whit repaired the snow walls around our campsite, Adrian and I shoveled the area clear of drifting snow until we had a smooth, level floor upon which to pitch our tents. In the meantime, Mike carved out a protected spot for our stove. Before long he had a kettle of snow melted for hot chocolate.

The next step in setting up the camp was carving out a restroom. In all my reading preparing for the hike, I'd never really thought about this very necessary facility. It consists of a seating area with a hole in the middle and a disposable plastic bag arranged beneath the hole. After use, the plastic bag is replaced by another. To dispose of the used bag, the team must rope up, walk to the edge of a deep crevasse, and toss the bag into it.

Usually the bag disappears from sight, never to be seen again. But if not, one must retrieve it and try again.

On one excursion, Mike needed to walk farther out onto the glacier to throw the bag out of sight while we waited, roped up, to guide him should he have any difficulty. On his trip back to secure ground, we heard a loud pop. The ground beneath us shifted a few inches. Afraid the ice beneath his feet was cracking and about to send him plummeting into a crevasse, Mike leapt to safety.

These crevasses are so breathtakingly beautiful—deep blue-green ice skirted by pristine white snow twisting and curving up a slope—it seemed a shame to pollute them. Especially with man-made plastic that would still be around a thousand years from now. However, realistically, there are no other options in a land of snow and ice.

The next day I stayed behind at the 10,000-foot camp while the rest of the team took a carry up to 11,200 feet. Even when my legs weren't injured or overtired, I had to take extra care to keep my stump strong and keep it from breaking down.

Lacking something better to do, I cleared a snow cave, big enough to walk inside and store our gear. I was adding the final touches to my creation when Rocky ambled over to our campsite.

We spent a few hours talking. Rocky, a ski bum from Aspen, Colorado, as well as a Princeton graduate, told me how he and Kelly, his climbing partner, had done pot while hiking on the mountain. He pushed his long, straggly hair away from his face. "Yeah, it was really cool, dude. A real trip."

"Weren't you afraid of stepping off into a crevasse or an avalanche?"

"Everything was cool. Besides we can handle the stuff, dude."

"I hope so," I said, "for your sake."

"So when do you plan to summit?" he asked.

"On June 1st."

He nodded his head in agreement. "That's cool. Hey, dude, I got a couple of ounces of marijuana. Do you want some?"

"Naw." I shook my head. "I don't use the stuff."

He studied the lighted joint perched between his thumb and middle finger. "Do you think this altitude could be really bad for me? I've been smoking dope all the way up the mountain."

I shrugged. "I'd quit if I were you."

"Thanks, dude, I think I will." He waved an idle hand.

I took a deep breath, filling my lungs with the cold, clean mountain air. I couldn't imagine taking drugs on a mountain climb. Besides the very real danger, it just seemed wrong. *This outdoor thing is about health and fresh air, being at one with nature and with God.*

When the team returned to camp that evening, I had a kettle of hot soup bubbling on the stove. Rocky and Kelly joined us around our camp stove. We talked late into the night about tomorrow's route, and Mike told stories about his Vietnam days.

The next morning Rocky stopped by our tent as we prepared for the climb to 11,200 feet. "Hey, dude, thought you might want to chow down on these leftovers."

Did we? Our eyes widened—our salivary glands shifted into overdrive. Rocky and Kelly were part of a well-respected guided climb in which the guides cook the meals for the climbers. We were grateful Rocky thought of us and our rehydrated oatmeal.

We roped up and hit the trail. The hike took an hour and a half. Once there, the team discussed continuing to the 14,000-foot camp before stopping. All three were impatient to summit the mountain.

"I think we should go on," Whit urged. "It's too soon in the day to stop and set up camp."

Adrian tapped the tip of his ski pole against a snow mound. "Yeah, I agree."

"I don't know." I eyed the cloud bank building to the west of us. "The park ranger recommended that climbers hike no more than 1,000 feet in elevation per day."

"That's just a guideline to go by, not a hard and fast rule," Mike drawled. His benign gaze masked his true feelings on the subject.

I shook my head. "I'm not comfortable with going on. I feel like God is telling me to take my time, not to rush the summit."

I couldn't miss hearing the corporate sigh from my teammates. Not being a professional climber like Mike or Adrian, I had to go with my instincts. They hadn't worked with any disabled persons before, so I had to be careful.

"I'd rather take an extra day doing the climb than risk anyone's safety. Besides, the ranger told us the storm could break at any time."

Whit and Adrian urged me to reconsider. Irritated, Mike slapped his gloves against his pant leg and strode away. While I knew that my decision irritated the others, I also knew that I had to listen to the inner Voice I'd come to know and to trust, despite the tension building between me and the rest of the team.

I don't know who first spotted the climbers coming down off the mountain. Shoulders drooping, hunched against the wind, they plodded like robots toward the camp, every step a chore. As they drew closer, I recognized the beard of Vern Tejas, a famous mountaineer and guide.

Suddenly I realized this team was the one I'd almost booked with a month ago. After praying about it, I didn't feel comfortable and decided to go with our own team.

"Hey," Adrian hailed them. "What happened? You guys look totally hammered."

"We are," one of the climbers replied, his face devoid of all animation, his eyes dulled by fatigue. "Got snowed in at the 17,200-foot camp for nine days. Lousy weather—forty below, high winds—miserable!"

"Did you summit?" Mike asked.

Another rough-looking climber, the energy beaten out of him, dropped his pack in the snow. "Naw, couldn't. The first break in the weather, and we high-tailed it for home." His voice belied his intense disappointment. He began setting up his camp beside ours. "I don't know what ever happened to the other team who went out before us. Never did see them again."

"Other team?" Whit strolled over to join the conversation.

"Yeah, the two Koreans. One's a park service employee and the other a trainee. They were just day climbing, off to the west of the primary route."

Mike took a sip form his mug. "Probably burrowed in on the mountain till the storm passed."

The climber frowned. "They weren't equipped for cold weather."

Seeing the worried look on my face, Adrian added, "I'm sure they're fine."

I sidled over to Vern Tejas. "Sir, are you, by any chance, Vern Tejas? The first man to winter solo Denali?"

The man straightened and eyed me respectfully. A grin spread across his worn and tired face. "You're quite observant."

He glanced down at my exposed artificial leg. "And you're that young hiker who's out to break the high points record. Sit down. Let's talk."

I stretched my hand out to meet his. "It's such an honor to meet you, sir. I've read about you in all the hiking journals. You're a legend."

The mountaineer studied my face for a moment. "And you, you're quickly becoming one. I can't tell you how much I admire you, to take on such a challenge as McKinley with only one leg. You'll have quite a story to tell your grandchildren someday."

I smiled with pleasure. "I believe everybody who attempts to overcome a difficult challenge in their lives has a story to tell. Like what you did today—surviving against the odds and making it down safely despite the storm. That was probably more of a challenge than summitting on a bright, sunny day."

"You're probably right."

I was glad when one of the members of his climbing team offered to take our picture together. I knew I would want to remember my encounter with one of the mountaineering greats.

"I saw a tape of you on 'Good Morning, America' a few days ago."

He grinned. "I suppose I'll be seeing you there in a few weeks."

I shrugged. "Maybe."

We talked for some time about the climb from which he had returned and I was about to take. I wished I had the courage to tell him of my fears. Somehow, I think he would have understood.

"No one is summitting right now," he said. "The windows in the storm aren't big enough to make it possible. Be smart when climbing the Great One. She's unforgiving. One miscalculation, and it's over." Then as an afterthought, he added, "Take your time."

I stared at the snow melting about the base of the camp stove's flickering flame. *Didn't summit. The team didn't summit. And I could have been with them. If I had been, the entire high point project would have been scrapped. I would never have been able to climb the mountain a second time and still complete the fifty high points to break the record.* I had prayed for wisdom at the time, and now, God seemed to be reassuring me once again of His leading.

CHAPTER FIFTEEN

Death on the Mountain

For six hours we hiked across huge crevasses and through freshly made avalanches. The narrow path pressed us from both sides. We rounded Windy Corner, toe by toe, and gazed down into the emerald crevasse. I marveled at the natural beauty of the mountain. For the first time since I'd begun the climb, I began to feel the strength of the Great One.

As I continued climbing, my breathing became more labored. Also, I was sweating even though it was bitterly cold. And I was drinking far more than normal. I began to worry about dehydration.

The 14,000-foot camp looked like a city, with people and tents everywhere. Whatever isolation I had felt earlier gave way to tents, radio antennas, the odors of food cooking, the sound of laughter, and the goings and comings of a helicopter.

Surely there is safety in numbers, I thought. Peace filled me; I sighed with relief. The stirrings in my stomach didn't quiet so easily. By the time we settled in for the night, my stomach rumbled and gurgled. I could hardly put one foot in front of the other. I told Whit, "I'm really tired. I think I may have altitude sickness."

He laughed and waved me away. "It's all in your head."

"I don't think so. Our rate of ascent today was sharp. I really feel miserable."

Mike overheard what I said. "Todd, you'll be fine. It won't be a problem, I assure you."

Adrian added his assurances. "There's nothing to worry about. I've been up and down mountains a dozen times or more and never once contracted acute mountain sickness. Besides, it's all in the head." He tapped his forehead.

"Tell it to my gut." I looked at my climbing partners with frustration and disgust. *At least you could be sympathetic*, I thought. *After all, I'm paying for this expedition!* "I'm going over to the ranger station. They have a medical doctor on duty."

The short walk to the ranger tent seemed interminable. The closer I got, the worse I felt. My thoughts flashed to our summit pitch. *If I have a bad case of AMS, the doctor will send me down the mountain to the hospital. It will end the climb. The entire project will be lost. All the planning, all the preparations, everything lost!* I stumbled into the ranger station and asked the ranger on duty, "How do you know if you have altitude sickness?"

The man eyed me critically for a moment. "Come around to the medical tent. There's a simple test we can administer that will measure the amount of oxygen in your blood."

I followed him to the round tent where the medical supplies were kept. "Got a possible AMS here for you, Doc," he called out.

The doctor, an emergency physician from Boulder, Colorado, gestured me toward the white metal stool. "So you're feeling kind of punk, huh?"

I nodded, telling him all my symptoms.

"Even been above 10,000 feet before?"

"Only in a jet plane."

He grinned. "Ya haven't lost your sense of humor, anyway. That's a good sign."

He put a clamp on my finger. A wire attached me to an instrument that flashed red digital numbers.

"Seventy-three. You have 73 percent of the required amount of oxygen necessary in your blood. You have a mild case of altitude sickness."

My heart dropped to my feet. Would this be the end of our climb?

He continued. "The good news is, it's mild enough so that we won't need to take any drastic measures. I have some pills for you to take that will increase your respiration, which, in turn, will pump more oxygen into your blood. Because of the side effects such as tingling in the fingers and frequent urination, I advise you to take only half a tablet and drink a lot of liquids. I'll give you enough to last for the rest of your climb."

I thanked the doctor and headed back to my camp. On the way I wondered if the symptoms would get worse the higher I climbed on the mountain. Still, I experienced a grim satisfaction when I told my teammates that my symptoms were real and not just in my head.

After drinking a cup of hot soup, I crawled into my sleeping bag, pulled the hood over my head, and slept the entire night. Often people have trouble sleeping at such high altitudes. I didn't. I got the best sleep of anyone that night. By morning I felt stronger, and my symptoms were gone. We spent the next two days in camp, getting used to the change in altitude before proceeding up the mountain.

It was noticeably colder than it had been at the lower altitudes. We chose a campsite and set to our individual chores. After Adrian and I cleared our spot and pitched the tents, we eagerly anticipated our reward, a cup of hot apple cider. While nursing the hot mugs between our stiff, chilled hands, we got acquainted with the other campers. At 8:00, we clustered around our portable radio to hear Ranger Annie give the weather forecast for the next two days.

"There is currently a low-pressure system on the mountain. It looks like it will last for another day. There is a possibility of a high-pressure system moving in behind it."

While we knew that the ranger forecasts were extremely conservative so as to keep people from taking unnecessary risks, we groaned at the news. Another day of bad weather at the summit!

We rested at the camp for two days. On the third day, the team made a carry up to 16,800 feet, where they stashed our cache in the snow. While the three of them were gone, I strolled over to the ranger tent and made friends with Jim. We sat around his tent, drinking hot chocolate and talking about the mountain and its many moods.

"You can't be too careful on old Denali," Jim warned. "A couple years back, a friend of mine, a climber from Poland, soloed to the summit. A storm hit as he started back down. He'd only gone one or two hundred feet from the top when he was forced to stop and dig a snow cave. Since he'd intended to make the summit in one day, he hadn't brought along his stove or the sleeping gear he needed to bivouac on the mountain."

No matter how often the rangers and the veteran climbers told their war stories, I listened with rapt attention. If I could learn the secrets of the mountain, maybe I could avoid trouble before it hit.

Jim continued. "No one had seen or heard from him since he hiked out of camp. On the third day the weather broke, and I immediately sent out an air rescue team. The pilot of the plane spotted him coming out of his snow cave—alive. They radioed to base for a helicopter to airlift him out.

"He lost both legs below the knee from frostbite." Jim cleared his throat. "He's living in Anchorage. Meeting you would be a real encouragement for him."

"Give me his name and phone number. I'll be glad to talk with him."

When the team returned to camp, Whit was feeling quite sick. The steepest part of the trail had been a rough climb. We discussed the possibility of waiting another day until Whit felt better.

"No," he insisted, "I'll be fine by morning."

Early the next morning we awakened to the roar of a helicopter circling overhead. I stuck my head out of the tent to see what was happening, but the low cloud ceiling obstructed my view of the chopper. I called to one of the hikers we had spoken with the night before. "What's happening out there?"

He paused, his eyes filled with anguish. "The two Koreans— the rescue team found them."

"And?" I knew without asking, but I had to ask anyway.

He shook his head and bit his lip. "It's bad. Really bad."

It's bad. Really bad. It's bad. Really bad. My hands shook as I crawled out of my sleeping bag and dug the clothing I would wear that day out from the bottom of my sleeping bag.

I strapped on my artificial leg and stuck my other foot into my plastic boot, which had frozen solid during the night. In case you didn't know, putting on a frozen boot is like putting your foot into a bag of ice cubes and walking around on them until they melt. My artificial leg wasn't much better.

Next to me, Whit grunted and burrowed deeper into his bag. Adrian, on the other side of Whit, sat up. "What's happening?"

"They found the Korean hikers." My voice caught in my throat. For even though I had never met the men, we were kin—brothers facing the same odds and possibly the same fate. "The chopper's coming to take their remains off the mountain."

I hopped out of the tent and hurried over to join the silent assembly of climbers watching the rescue team load the two black body bags into the helicopter. I shuddered as the helicopter lifted off, one body bag draped over the pilot's lap for the entire flight off the mountain.

"Imagine flying all the way to Anchorage with a dead body resting in your lap," I whispered.

One of the veteran climbers kicked at the snow by his feet. "Sometimes, when they can't fly in to retrieve the bodies, the rangers have to store them in the snow until it's safe for the chopper to land."

"What happened to them?" I asked the man nearest me.

"As much as the rangers can piece together, the storm moved in, and the two climbers didn't have the necessary gear with them. So instead of hunkering down to weather out the storm, they headed back across Head Wall." He swallowed hard. "One stepped into a crevasse. They found him dangling from his rope, upside down. The other man was sitting on a rock, holding his radio next to his head. Both were frozen to death."

Rocky caught up to me on the way back to our campsite. "Man, what a bummer."

I nodded but couldn't reply. I couldn't stop thinking of the two men's families and the grief they would soon be experiencing. The faces of my mom and dad surfaced before my eyes. I knew that they anxiously waited for news of my successful ascent of the Great One. All the doubts I'd had before beginning the climb returned, bringing along with them a retinue of gruesome new considerations.

Before long, however, the words of my friends Fred and Kathy came back to me.

"You'll do fine, Todd," Fred encouraged when I talked to him about McKinley. "The head wall is steep, but you can make it."

Kathy seconded his thoughts. "You're going to be fine, Todd. Just go up there and have fun on the mountain."

I thought of all the comfort and encouragement Lisa had given me when I called her from the 7,000-foot base camp. *What friends! I am so blessed.* I choked back a wave of emotions and turned my gratitude toward my best Friend, who had come with me every step of the way. I recited His words of encouragement aloud as I dressed for the climb. "Lo, I am with you always, even unto the ends of the earth."

"Unto the ends of the earth." I stared off in the direction of the North Peak and smiled to myself. "Ya gotta' admit, Father, Mount McKinley definitely qualifies as the 'ends of the earth!' "

CHAPTER SIXTEEN

17,000 Feet High

A somber atmosphere permeated our camp that night. I kept seeing those body bags as I prepared to sleep. *It could have been me. It still could be—maybe tomorrow.*

Whit, especially, had been quieter than usual since the helicopter left. As we climbed into our sleeping bags, he said, "You know, seeing those body bags today sure brings it home to you how dangerous it really is up there."

I looked at him in surprise. This was "go-get-'em" Whit talking. "You're right," I said. I felt more nervous than ever.

After a quiet breakfast the next morning, we roped up—Mike in front, me, Whit, then Adrian on the end. Gliding my hand over the metal climbing gear, I adjusted the harness around my waist for comfort. The sled loaded with our gear and food rode along behind Adrian.

With great effort, we began up the mountain. The low ceiling of clouds had lifted, and for the first time, we saw the other side of the mountain. Row upon row of mountains and valleys stretched eastward, all lathered with snow and glistening in the midday sun.

Far up ahead, the people climbing Head Wall looked like a row of ants carrying food back to their hill. However, any levity that image conjured up disappeared when we passed the spot where the bodies of the two Koreans had been discovered.

My confidence grew as we traversed up the Head Wall. We used ascenders on the ropes installed by the guide services to ice climb up the slope. We were moving at a fast pace, but Mike wanted to move faster. He had set the goal of reaching the 17,000-foot base camp before quitting for the day.

Surrounded by majesty, I felt insignificant and fragile beyond words when I reached the base of the West Buttress. To me, the mountain represented a power and a force too awesome and great for humans, a spiritual experience too intricate to describe. I decided that the mastery of the peaks took more than a sound heart and lungs. To drive the legs and body beyond the fatigue level took a personal resolve, a determination, a positive inner spirit or force.

As I began the toe-to-toe climb along that steep ridge, I realized that it wasn't the excitement of climbing the high peaks or the flirtation with danger that motivated me. It was the desire to challenge the walls that society, or perhaps I, myself, had built around me.

Here in the mountains I was learning how I could discover myself—the limits to my endurance, the power that resides in my innermost being, and the spirit that can drive me beyond those limitations.

For days I had watched from a distance as hikers traveled up and down the Head Wall. As I got closer, it seemed even more formidable—especially with that yawning crevasse at the base. Just in case you slip and fall.

Toe by toe, inch by inch, I moved, the dull thud of the ice ax securing each step or pulling my weight up to the next level. We edged along the ridge of rock and wind-packed snow on our way to the 17,000-foot level. I tried to remain focused, to always be guarding against any misstep that could lead to defeat and destruction—not easy to do looking into the jaws of a crevasse.

The shortage of oxygen and the constant pressure on my stump pounded the strength out of me. I was exhausted. My inner voice warned me to stop and rest. "Todd, you shouldn't go on to the 17,000. You need to get acclimatized. You're not ready for it." I remembered Vern's and Jim's warnings, "Take it slow."

After climbing another 1,000 feet, I decided to heed their warnings. "I've got to take a break," I called. I could see by the disappointed looks on my teammates' faces that they found my exhaustion inconvenient.

With the wind off another glacier whipping up the side of the mountain in a frenzy, I found a rock where I could rest. My tongue felt as though it had been swabbed with a cotton ball. I took a swig from my water bottle, savoring the relief the cold liquid gave my throat. We had just passed the 16,000-foot side of a ridge by a hundred feet or so.

"Don't go on any farther today," the voice inside said again. Everything in me cried, "Stop!" I glanced about for a place to camp. I knew without being told that the area was too exposed to the elements for setting up a safe camp.

"Adrian," I confided, "I don't feel I can go on any farther. It isn't that I'm blown out, but I think I need to take it slower. I need to conserve my leg for the summit."

"Look, Todd, I need to get back. I can't take much more time off from work to do this climb."

"I know, but I just feel it's important that we not move too fast." I tried to explain my reasoning. "Think about it. There are two advantages to setting up camp here. If a storm materializes, we'll be much safer here. All we would have to do is bolt down the ropes as quickly as possible and hurry down to the 14,000-foot camp, where the rangers are there to help us. But if we climbed the last 1,000 feet, Whit and I would be weaker from our altitude sickness. We might not be able to make it back to the safety of the 14,000-foot camp."

"And the second?"

"The second is, if the storm doesn't materialize, we'll be starting out fresh and ready for that last push to the summit."

He passed on the word to Whit and Mike. Grudgingly, Mike stopped, leaned on his ice ax, and heaved an exasperated sigh. "We'd better go back, then," he said, "to the 16,000-foot level."

We turned around and trudged back down. As we were setting up camp, the Peter Pan Expedition passed by on their way up. I couldn't miss the yearning in my teammates' eyes as they watched the other team disappear up the trail.

That evening we sat in the big tent and listened to the radio. The weather service reported a Baltic storm coming in. Baltic storms can continue for four or five days. I remembered hearing about thirteen climbers who died in such a storm last year. I knew that if the weather got bad while we were camping at 17,000 feet, we would have a shortage of food, but by camping at the 16,000-foot level, we could drop down below the head wall and get more food from our stash if necessary.

We awakened to a total whiteout. Except for the constant whistle of the wind, we were trapped in a colorless, silent, surrealistic world of vacuous white. We had nowhere to go and nothing to do but stay in our tents, wrapped up in our sleeping bags.

The hours passed slowly. Occasionally, hikers stumbled down from the 17,000-foot level. Their comments were all the same. "It's miserable up there! Much colder! The winds could blow you off the side of the mountain. We're bailing out!" They were afraid that they didn't have enough food to wait out the storm.

The Peter Pan Expedition team members trudged back into camp with someone from another team who had severely injured his hip. He had to be carried down to the 14,000-foot level, where he would be airlifted off the mountain. I drank my hot cider and felt saddened by the evidence of disappointment and defeat in the men's faces. To me, they were true heroes by choosing to rescue another climber instead of summitting.

Before they left for the 14,000-foot camp, one of the Peter Pan Expedition members gave us their extra cache of food. Other returning groups did the same rather than carrying the added weight down the mountain or abandoning it to the elements. For us, every little bit helped. And saved money for future climbs.

One guy who had climbed all forty-nine other high points trudged by. "McKinley is not my mountain. I'm going home!" He was one mountain shy of having hiked the fifty states!

As I trudged back to our campsite, I thought about the

storm and the hopes that had been dashed by it. *If we don't make it to the top, the entire Summit America Expedition is a bust! And we can't wait up here forever for the storm to pass.*

The oppressive feelings I'd had since seeing the Koreans' bodies being airlifted off the mountain pervaded my mind until my thoughts seemed disjointed and unreal.

Alone in the tent, I fell to my knees. *If I have to turn back now, without making it to the top . . .* "Oh, God, has it all been in vain? I can't believe we've come this far to turn back now. Please give us what we need to make it to the top. I'm not asking You to do the work for me; just give me the opportunity to do it."

That night the temperatures dropped. To lighten our packs, we had chosen to leave Mike's tent with our stash at the 14,000-foot base camp, so all four of us piled into the three-man tent. Whit, Adrian, and I slept feet to head while Mike stretched out across the bottom of the tent. Cramped by the crowded conditions, I lay motionless in my sleeping bag for several hours, unable to get comfortable or to turn off the troublesome thoughts of the day.

We awoke to cloudless blue skies and pristine white snow—a perfect day for climbing.

"It's a short climb today," Adrian assured me as I adjusted my crampon onto my plastic boot.

After roping up, we headed for the ridge. We used our ice axes for self-arrest and the guide services' ropes and cinders wherever available. I paused at one point to catch my breath. Adrian and Whit drew closer. Mike waited up ahead. We had met a few other climbers along the way, but mainly, the mountain was ours to enjoy.

I gazed down the sharp drop-off from the ridge to the valley below. I appreciated being roped up to three other people who could stop my fall. "Are we almost there?" I asked as I took a long drink from my water bottle.

"Oh, yeah, it's not far now," both Whit and Adrian assured me.

"Good." I tucked my water bottle into my pack and set out once more. Each time I stopped to rest, they gave me the same answer, "It's not far. We're almost there."

After the third or fourth time, I finally caught on and stopped believing them. *Am I ever glad,* I mused as I righted myself after another fall, *I didn't let them talk me into doing this the other day after we had already climbed so far!*

Hours later, we reached the 17,000-foot base camp. My head ached enough from the higher altitude to take some pain medication, but I couldn't do that until we stopped to make camp. At the edge of the camp, I looked about in surprise. It was a ghost camp. The snow walls surrounded empty spaces instead of clusters of tents. All except one climbing team had bailed out yesterday after the storm. *If only they had known what a great day they would have today for climbing!*

While Whit, Adrian, and I set up camp, Mike feverishly tried to light the stove. Lack of oxygen and the strong winds kept it from lighting. Without a stove to melt snow for drinking water and food, we would be in deep trouble. I tried not to appear anxious during the half-hour he worked over it.

I guess the others were doing the same, because all four of us breathed a sigh of relief when the burner finally caught fire. The cup of hot chocolate I savored minutes later tasted better than any I could remember.

The exhaustion and stress led to shorter tempers than usual. That, added to disagreements about climbing strategy, elevated the tension between us.

Later, in the tent, our crowded quarters seemed even more crowded than the night before. No one was in the mood to swap stories. As I stared up at the dome over our heads, watching it frost over with our breath, my thoughts returned to my original fear.

Is tomorrow my last day? Will we summit? I shut my eyes and burrowed deep into my sleeping bag. Next to me, Whit grunted in his sleep. Adrian mumbled some unintelligible words. Mike nudged my foot as he shifted his weight. All three were asleep, and I was wide awake.

I pulled out the tape recorder that had been my faithful companion. "Tomorrow is it," I whispered into my cassette recorder so as not to disturb the others. Above my face, the tent dome billowed and shuddered in the howling sub-Arctic winds. "They're calling for a major storm. But, as yet, the sky has been clear and blue—a perfect day for a summit pitch."

Turning off my recorder, I stowed it safely in my pack. A light dusting of snow descended on my shoulders and the top of my head like dandruff falling on a black wool suit. During the night, the condensation from our breathing froze on the nylon dome of our tent, becoming snow when disturbed. I ignored it and burrowed deep into my sleeping bag.

When morning finally arrived, we ate breakfast and prepared for the day's climb. Conversation was kept to a minimum.

In spite of the tension, I was pumped. This was the big day! I leaned back and gazed at the sky over my head—perfect! My stomach churned with anticipation.

By 8:30 we were on the trail. Mike set a fast pace across a long snow field; Adrian and Whit followed. Stressed about the dissension and bickering, I plodded behind them, falling farther and farther behind. My enthusiasm disappeared like the fog. I couldn't seem to concentrate on my climbing. Noticing how far ahead of me they had gotten, I tried to match their pace but couldn't.

We had crossed 200 yards of the field when I stopped and stuck my ice ax into the snow. "Hey! Remember me?" I shouted. "Remember the reason we're climbing this mountain?"

The three men turned, shrugged, and trudged back to where I stood.

"Look, we can't go on climbing this way. We're out of sync with one another. We need to operate as a team." I steadied myself on the handle of my ice ax. "You're setting too fast a pace, guys. I can't do it."

"Well," Mike pursed his lips, "if you feel like you're not able to make it, the three of us can go on to the top without you. With Whit completing every climb, you could still say the Summit America Expedition had set a new fifty-peaks record."

"No!" I shook my head vehemently. "It wouldn't be the same if Whit alone climbs all fifty high points. The object of the climb is for a disabled person to do all fifty. Don't you see?" I searched their eyes for understanding. "The message I'm trying to send is that no challenge is impossible to overcome with determination and with God on your side."

Adrian tightened his mouth into a thin line. "I don't know . . ."

"It only works if I, an amputee climber, not an able-bodied climber, make it to the top. Don't you see? This is more than just another climb or another record broken. And you three, your job is to see that the goal is reached!"

I could tell by their stony faces that my message wasn't getting through. I took a deep breath and set my jaw. "We've got to get this right, or I'm turning around right here and now!"

I had considered the risks and decided I had little choice. "I'm serious! Either you gauge your pace to mine and we work as a team, or it's over."

CHAPTER SEVENTEEN

Summit!

Several moments of silence passed. I read the expressions on Whit's, Adrian's, and Mike's faces and sensed that they were struggling. We all knew that if I decided to turn back, one of them would have to return with me, leaving only two to complete the climb, a dangerous journey under the best of circumstances, and foolish, considering the storms passing through the area. If we turned back now, there wouldn't be another chance to summit.

Adrian exhaled sharply. "OK, we'll keep going. Anytime you want to slow down or turn around, we'll do it."

"Fine. Then the team's motivating factor must be that everyone complete the ascent, right?" I searched each of their faces for answers.

Mike and Whit mumbled their consent.

"Great! Let's get going."

Throughout the climb to the top of Denali Pass, Mike set an easy pace. We rested at the top, then continued up a short, extremely icy slope. As we crossed the area known as Football Field, we talked about being the first team to summit on June 1st. We groaned when another team passed us halfway across the field.

At the other side, I stopped and stared up. "Is that it?" I asked.

"That's it," Mike answered. "Pig Hill."

Pig Hill, with its steep slope and razor edge, would be a killer at any altitude. But at 19,000 feet? It seemed impossible. *I can do this,* I told myself. *I have to.*

On the way up the eastern slope of Pig Hill, an aching numbness crept into my back muscles. My good leg throbbed with pain. My stump did the same. I pushed the pain to the back of my mind and concentrated on putting one foot in front of the other. My body cried out for relief, but there was nowhere to stop, nowhere to rest.

Leaning against my ice ax, I thought, *God wants me to do this—the message must get out. If I don't make it, no one will ever know.*

Before long, I had a formula. *Take three breaths, step, stop and rest. Take three breaths, step, stop and rest.* Over and over I repeated the pattern. *So many steps . . . step . . . breathe . . . stop . . . and rest.*

The lack of oxygen took its toll on my body. Extreme fatigue quivered deep inside me like Jell-O congealing in a mold. I inhaled a ragged gulp of air.

My good leg floundered like cooked linguini; my stump like vermicelli. I hated the slow going. My mind schemed to scramble up the side of the wall like a kid scaling monkey bars; my body mocked the very idea. Pushed beyond anything I had imagined during all my months of training, the wicked wall threatened to break me.

I willed my legs to become impersonal objects, unattached to the rest of me. Hauling the ax out of the snowbank, I slammed it into a higher point on the wall and took another step. My heart pounded against my chest. An unseen power forced the air from my chest. I slammed the ax against the mountain again. *You will not win,* I challenged. *You will not destroy me!* I took another labored step. Each step, I set my jaw and repeated, *I have to make it to the top!*

I wrestled all thoughts of defeat and death from my mind with the promises I had learned as a child. "God is my strength and my fortress!" I tried to see past the white wall in front of me. The words of a fellow hiker echoed in my brain.

"Pig Hill is really tough, takes everything out of you, a purely psychological battle to get yourself up there. Once you get to the top, you look ahead and go, 'Wow!' You see a whole other climb the summit."

Winning the war sounded so cerebral sitting around a camp stove and drinking hot chocolate. Now I knew what real cold, real pain, really was.

"Don't get discouraged. The last thrust is deceiving. It's really only a short walk, even though it looks long. Get past Pig Hill, and the rest is easy."

The rest is easy. The rest is easy. Get past Pig Hill. The rest is easy. Setting my jaw, I kept my eyes on the trail and my mind on taking the next step. Step after step after step after step, I clambered toward the top of the wall. With every step of the last hundred yards, a grenade of pain exploded in my legs. Then I post-holed and fell.

It hurt to breathe the cold air—it burned my nose like the tubes had after my boating accident. Breathing through my mouth turned it into cotton. The results of a runny nose were frozen to my face mask.

I won't quit! I won't give up! I struggled to my feet and leaned with both hands on my ice ax in knee-deep snow. *I have to make it! I have to do whatever it takes. If I don't, the message God gave me will never, ever be heard!*

With each step, a fresh spasm of hot pain exploded in my foot. Another seared the end of my stump. My lungs threatened to burst with my every breath. My heartbeat drummed against my temples to the rhythm of my pain.

At the moment I knew I could go no farther, Whit pointed ahead. "There's the summit, over there."

I gazed in awe at what lay ahead. The summit seemed indomitable. "We still have to go that much higher and farther?"

Then I remembered the climber's words. "It's just an easy walk."

And it was. Whether due to the gradual ascent or the adrenaline pulsating through my body, I maintained a slow, but steady pace along the ridge at 20,000 feet. A world of sunshine, blue sky, and sparkling snow spread out before me.

As I walked, I identified the different mountain ranges, from Alaska's flat areas to the Alaskan Range, Mount McKinley, and the Bowl. Behind was the North Peak, 850 feet shorter than the South Peak toward which I was heading. Separated by the Harper Glacier, the two peaks stand about 3.5 miles apart.

To the west of us, fat, puffy clouds billowed over the horizon. While they looked friendly, I knew that within a half-hour's time, we could be trapped in a life-or-death situation. At that altitude, there was no mercy. Yet, somehow, I knew the storm would not reach us.

The exquisite scenery infused me with the energy to keep walking. Step after step, the tension within me built as the summit loomed closer. My artificial foot slipped off the path. I struggled to my feet and continued climbing. Up ahead, Mike turned and raised his hands in triumph. He had reached the summit.

I accelerated my pace.

"Here it is!" Mike shouted.

I lunged up the last few feet of the mountain. My eyes caught the glint from the flags left by previous expeditions, announcing the high point of North America.

"Yeah! Thank God!" My shout filled every crevasse and canyon in Denali National Park. Dizzy from the altitude and the victory, I took a deep breath. The bitter cold air rumbled through my lungs, then out again. I had made it! I had accomplished my goal—I had conquered the highest and the roughest of the mountains!

If I live to be 125, I will never forget the moment I reached the South Summit. Dizzy with excitement, I posed for pictures. *William Todd Huston! You did it!* By the grace of God, I'd beaten the odds. A wave of emotion washed over me, and my eyes filled with tears. I swallowed hard and looked away from Mike. Even after inhaling several times, I still wasn't much in control of my feelings.

I was standing on the top of Mount McKinley, on top of the entire continent of North America!

CHAPTER EIGHTEEN

The Hard Road Down

As far as the eye could see, sun glinted off the snow in a progression of blues, grays, and whites. Wanting never to forget the experience, I tried to imprint on my mind the incredible sight of hundreds of square miles sprawling at my feet, of mountain after snowcapped mountain dominating the horizon.

Then Mike stepped up beside me. "This makes it all worth it, huh?"

I searched my brain for an adequate gesture or word to express myself. I couldn't find anything that came close to the numb happiness I felt. This high place represented so many goals and ambitions, I could barely even think straight. To share the depth of the emotions I was feeling at that moment seemed like an invasion of my privacy.

My moment of introspection faded when the rest of the team joined us. Adrian thumped me on the back. "You've done it. The hardest mountain is won. You have a great chance to break my record."

He was right. My chances of success with the remaining mountains were much better now that I had the experience of climbing McKinley—the highest mountain, not only in Alaska, not only in the United States, but in all of North America.

Exuberant over our victory, the four of us danced and shouted in the snow like the varsity football team after defeating the high school's arch enemy at the homecoming game.

Maybe it was just the excitement, but suddenly I wasn't cold at all. "I expected it would be much colder up here," I called to Mike.

He glanced down at the thermometer on his pack. "It's not bad, only ten degrees."

"Above or below zero?" I asked.

"Below."

"You're right, Todd. It feels warmer than that to me," Whit agreed, wiping his gloved hand across his nose. He found the mucous from his nose frozen on his face. "I guess it's pretty cold after all."

I began to shiver from the sweat I had worked up during the climb, sweat that was already chilling my body. *Maybe beautiful, but not a friendly place for man or beast,* I thought.

"We'd better not stay here too long." Mike drove his ice ax into the snow by his feet. "Let's get a few more snapshots and head back down before the next storm hits."

We shot a number of photographs of one another holding victory banners and of the summit and the spectacular scenery surrounding us. Every direction I looked brought a new rush of emotion. *If only this moment could last.* I never wanted this moment to slip from my memory.

Fifteen minutes after our arrival, the frigid temperatures seeped through our Arctic-tested clothing, convincing us that we were visitors, not residents. It was time to begin the long descent back toward civilization.

I took one last 360-degree pan of the world atop Mount McKinley. My eyes misted to match the smile that spread across my face. Momentarily speechless, I stared at the frozen world, sprawling in muted splendor beneath me. For a moment, nothing else stirred. I breathed deeply, then let it out slowly as the solitude of the mountain engulfed me. The whine of a light breeze soothed my senses, lulling me into an exquisite sense of contentment and peace. It was as if the entire world were holding its breath for us.

All the months of hard work—for me, for Lisa, for Whit—it was worth it. All the people who have been praying for me— Thank You, God, for answering those prayers!

For all the exhilaration I felt conquering the highest point in North America, it wouldn't mean much if I didn't make it back to civilization alive. And really, I was only halfway there. I still had to climb down the mountain. And with my energy drained and my legs in bad shape, it wouldn't be easy.

The trip down would be a lot shorter—only two days, compared to the twelve-day ascent.

I didn't realize the extent of my exhaustion until I took my first steps downward. If I thought my legs were like boiled noodles before . . . now I had a whole new definition of pain and pasta.

My stump screamed from the pain of each step. The muscles in my other leg responded in perfect synchronization. Gritting my teeth, I focused my thoughts on one step at a time.

We completed the first part of the descent quickly and with relative ease. Then we started down the infamous Pig Hill. A few steps, then, *squish*. My artificial leg post-holed into the snow. Before I could recover my balance, the trail broke away, propelling me sideways down the wall.

In a blur I flailed the air, grabbing for the rope attached to my climbing belt. *Why isn't the rope holding me?* I could sense my falling body gaining speed. Snow-sky-snow-sky! I tumbled faster and faster.

"Whoa!" I could hear my climbing partners shouting.

It's all over, I thought, with a moment of detachment, *So, this is what it's like to . . .*

Suddenly, the rope jerked taut. I skidded to a stop and, for a moment, stared at the cascades of loose snow tumbling down into the valley. Recovering my senses, I jammed the ice ax into the snow pack and hauled myself back onto the trail.

Too tired to exalt, I rested for a moment, my breath coming in short, agonizing spurts. Pain shot through my legs as I struggled to my feet. Laboriously, I lifted my artificial leg and took a step, then another. Step in front of step in front of step.

Suddenly, I post-holed again. Again I tumbled from the trail. Rolling onto my stomach, I fought my way to my feet once more, only to tumble again. My pack hung heavy on my shoulders. A numb aching crept into the muscles up and down my spine. The small pain in my eyes increased to industrial strength. I longed to stop, to take a break.

The day's sunlight had softened the snow on the trail so that every few steps, my artificial leg post-holed through the crust, spewing my body down the mountainside. After each fall, I struggled to my feet, focusing my attention on the trail before me. I wanted to pray for strength, but the pain in my body overrode my thinking process.

I knew I couldn't stop—not now. Not with the knowledge that I'd made it to the summit, that I'd conquered my doubts, waged a war inside my head—a war against my body's cries of protest, its demands for an unconditional surrender.

I smiled through my pain. The grueling pace continued. The shin muscles on my good leg ached like the infected nerve on an abscessed tooth. The contact point between my stump and the artificial limb throbbed with a pain so intense that I dreaded each step.

Just one more step, I told myself. But as I took it, my artificial leg post-holed again, pitching me face-first into the snow. Saturated with sweat and in agony, I rolled over and wiped the snow from my goggles. I looked at the sapphire blue sky above me, defeated.

I never want to get up again, I thought. *I can't, God. I can't go on any longer.* Through blurred eyes, I gazed at endless white-capped mountain peaks. That's when another text I had memorized as a child came like a soothing breeze to my mind. "Call upon me in the day of trouble, and I will deliver you."

Deliver me? Off the mountain? In what, an extraterrestrial helicopter? Like Elijah's chariot? That's what it would take, Lord.

Above me, I could hear Mike's and Adrian's voices. "Todd, are you all right? Did you break something? What's the matter with you?"

But a louder, more insistent voice overrode their concerns. "I will lift up mine eyes unto the hills—my help cometh from the Lord, the Maker of heaven and earth. He will not let your foot slip."

Slip? Slip, Lord? That's all I've been doing down the entire mountain—slipping, falling, and getting up, only to slip again!

"He will not let your foot slip." The message was clear and distinct. Deep in my mind, in utter despair, I cried, *Oh, God, help me. Help me now!*

CHAPTER NINETEEN

Cheers Through the Pain

One more step, I told myself. *I've got to get up and take one more step.*

When I got up, determined to take another step, something changed inside of me. Call it a second wind, an attitude adjustment, or whatever. It was as if my mind divorced my body and the pain that was wracking it. All thoughts of quitting vanished. All thoughts of failure disappeared.

I still hurt, and hurt badly, but it was as if an outside source of energy propelled me slowly, steadily down the trail. Slipping, sliding on my bottom, post-holing, the snow buildup on the points of my crampons, all that remained the same. What had changed was me.

When we reached Denali Pass, Mike set up snow stakes to act as anchors to control our descent. This was the spot where the soldier and his girlfriend had fallen after their summit. We climbed carefully down the slope. No one was in the mood for risks.

As we neared the 17,000-foot base camp, Adrian stayed to walk with me while Whit and Mike hurried ahead to start the camp stove and get the water boiling for hot drinks.

When I trudged the last few steps into camp, I was wiped out. Tossing my gear to the ground, I heaved a gigantic groan and fell onto my sleeping bag.

During the next hour, I groaned every five or ten seconds from the pain pulsating through my body with every heart-beat. I couldn't remember ever being in so much pain. I took a couple Advil tablets and burrowed down inside my sleeping bag.

One last conscious thought nagged at me as I drifted off to sleep. *How in the world will I ever be ready to climb the rest of the way down tomorrow?*

I fell asleep only to be awakened by the whine of an air-plane buzzing our tent. I looked at my watch. *It's 3:00 a.m. What is he buzzing our tent for at 3:00 a.m.?*

Later, I learned that a climber from a group on another route to the top developed cerebral edema, a swelling on the brain caused by the high altitude. Once again I felt blessed and protected.

The next morning, when I crawled out of the tent, I felt good, really good. I stretched my arms—no pain. I twisted my torso from side to side—no pain. I felt no pain in my back muscles. I flexed my good leg—no pain. I massaged my stump, still no pain. I was ready to roll.

We roped up, adjusted our crampons, and headed toward our first goal of the day, the 14,000-foot level. It was hard going. We had lots of exposure going down the head wall, but I soon adjusted to the rhythm. I couldn't walk sideways down the head wall like the other guys because my crampons wouldn't stay attached to my artificial foot. I solved the prob-lem by backing down the mountain, all the while hoping I wouldn't accidentally step into one of the hidden crevasses.

We took it slow across the ice field and down the avalanche area. Cautiously, we circumvented the open crevasses and finally arrived, safe and alive, at the 14,000-foot base camp. I threw my hands into the air and gave an Oklahoma cheer. What a great feeling it was to be back in civilization again! While Whit and the others set up camp, I shed my gear, hauled on my down-filled jacket, and walked to the ranger's tent.

"Hey, Jim," I called from outside his entryway.

"Come on in."

I didn't need a second invitation. I burst into the tent, shout-ing, "We did it! We summitted."

Jim leapt up from the table where he and three guests were dining. "Wonderful!" he shouted with a high-five slap.

I beamed all over. "It's incredibly beautiful up there, man." I couldn't believe how limited my vocabulary was when describing the experience.

"I told you. There's nothing like it. You'll never be the same again."

"You got that right. Hey, can I make a phone call from here?"

"You bet. Make yourself comfortable." He offered me a chair and returned to his meal and his guests.

Using my cellular telephone, I called Lisa. I could barely control my excitement when I heard her answer the phone from my apartment on Balboa Island in California.

"Lisa? We did it! We made it!"

"What?" I could picture her standing by the sink in the kitchen, holding a glass of mineral water in her hand.

"I said, we made it! We're back at 14,000 feet. We did it! Can you believe it?" I choked back a wave of emotion.

"Congratulations! I never doubted for a minute that you'd make it! But hey, that was fast. I didn't expect to hear from you for another week. And you're calling me directly from the mountain? You're crazy!" She laughed.

"God gave us the power and the strength to do it. It was a team effort and we did it." I loved repeating the words, *we did it.* "Can you call everyone, my folks, Fred and Kathy, and well, you know who?"

"Sure, I'll be glad to. I knew you could do it!" she repeated.

Good ol' Lisa. I tried to describe the climb—the beauty, the cold, the summit—but how can you make someone who hasn't been there understand?

After Lisa and I said goodbye, Jim invited me to eat with them. "I'm sure you're hungry for real food by now."

I hesitated. "Are you sure you have enough?"

"Are you kidding? We have plenty. Come on. Pull up your chair and tell us about your climb."

The warm and cozy atmosphere in the heated tent, plus the tantalizing aroma of hot macaroni and cheese, melted my resolve to return to my camp. Real food! I couldn't resist.

The five of us talked for more than three hours. I shared

my goals and challenges with the group. One of the ranger's guests talked about the challenges he was facing. The women talked about their search for identity and what they planned to do with their lives. At one point, I remembered my team-mates back at our camp.

When I mentioned my concern, Jim assured me, "They're welcome to join us. I still have plenty of leftovers."

But by the time I returned to the tent, they'd eaten their freeze-dried grub and were sleeping. I climbed into my bag and closed my eyes, expecting gentle waves of sleep to wash over me. Instead, I couldn't turn off the memories of the last few days on the mountain. I remembered what Jim had said about never being the same again. *He was right!* I smiled to myself as I thought of my friends and family members who had encouraged me to "go for it."

Then the face of my ex-wife surfaced in my mind. I winced. A hard knot of pain filled my throat. "Oh, God," I breathed. As quickly as the prayer escaped my lips, a fresh new thought replaced it. *Jessie gained a country, but you gained the world.*

The interviews I had done and all the speaking engagements I had waiting for me when I finished flashed to mind. *I really have gained the world. Who knows how far God will take this adventure?*

Morning arrived too soon. Our goal was to beeline it for the Kahiltna Glacier base camp. At first, it was slow going. The two sleds that were piled high with our gear kept sliding off the trail. We had to stop repeatedly to right the sleds and lift them back onto the trail. We did all this while roped together.

The sun rose in the sky, growing hotter as we descended the mountain. Snow melting on the glaciers created huge roll-ing hills of snow where flat, level terrain had been earlier. We had to skirt the places where climbers had punched holes into hidden crevasses along the trail. We could see places where hikers had fallen through, into crevasses, and then been rescued.

"Look, this is taking forever," Mike announced. "Let's cut the rope. Todd and I will move ahead on one rope, while you two use the other to maneuver the sleds down the mountain."

"Good idea." Adrian snapped out his pocket knife. "Once

we're past this section and pick up our last cache of supplies at 11,000 feet, the sleds will run better, and we'll be able to catch up with you in no time."

Mike and I trudged down Motorcycle Hill. We were moving faster, covering more ground. As soon as it was safe, I stopped to remove my crampons. My good leg was getting sore from jamming against the toe of my plastic boots. Without the traction, however, I slipped and slid down the rest of the slope.

My foot throbbed with pain. I cried out with each step. On and on, I limped. I had to stop at regular intervals to allow the blood to circulate in my foot. I appreciated how kind and patient Mike was with these delays.

Whit and Adrian caught up with us at 10,000 feet. "We'll keep going," Adrian suggested, "and set up camp at the 8,000-foot level."

I could only nod. The pain in my foot made speaking too much trouble. As they went on, I stumbled and fell to the ground. Mike helped me to my feet. "Todd," he said, "I'm sorry about all that up there on the mountain."

"Hey, man, you've more than made up for everything today. I appreciate the way you stuck by me. I couldn't have made it without you."

On our way down Ski Hill, we met Brian Okinek, another famous climber. He and the team he was leading clapped and cheered for me when we arrived at the 8,000-foot camp. There we threw our sleeping bags on the snow and slept for four hours. At 3:00 a.m., we headed down the slope and hiked the rest of the way on the Kahiltna Glacier while the snow was harder and easier to walk on.

When we arrived at the Kahiltna Glacier base camp, I headed straight for the ranger station. "Annie!" I burst through the front door. "We did it! We summitted."

"Hey!" The brown-haired woman with the giant smile leapt up from her desk at the radio controls and gave me a hug. "Congratulations! I heard it from Jim this morning."

We talked a few minutes about the climb. "Guess you'll be needing a taxi, huh?" Her eyes sparkled with happiness.

"Yup, this morning if possible. Whit and Adrian should be here any minute."

Annie seated herself in front of the shortwave radio and called the air taxi service at the Talkeetna International Airport. "Four more to transport, Jeff."

"Roger."

I waved to Annie and headed out the door. I had walked but a few feet when a stranger accosted me. "Hey, aren't you the guy I saw on the news?"

Others joined him.

"Congratulations!"

"Inspiring!"

"Great job!"

Every few feet, I posed for pictures with people I had never met before, people from around the world. They spoke to me in tongues I could not understand. However, their happiness in my victory transcended our language barriers.

Whit and Adrian arrived at the base camp a half-hour behind us. Since the weather was good, there were no flight delays. Only a strong wind whipped across the wide glacier.

Mike and I boarded the first plane; Whit and Adrian, the second. We taxied down the runway, the plane's wings quaking in the wind.

"Come on, baby," the pilot coaxed. "Don't do this to me, baby. Hold 'er for me. You can do it!"

I glanced nervously at the pilot, then at Mike. Had I come this far, only to crash into the icy glacier? Would the memory of our victory be only a footnote in the Anchorage newspaper's obituary column?

CHAPTER TWENTY

On to Rainier

The plane slid and bounced from side to side, then straightened and lifted up into the air. I breathed a sigh of relief. We were finally on our way to Talkeetna and civilization! The camp at Kahiltna Glacier grew smaller and smaller the higher we climbed. I strained my neck to catch the last glimpse of the mountain I had grown to love, dangers and all. McKinley had given me so much.

I closed my eyes and tried to imagine which of society's little conveniences I had missed most. Many things entered my mind: being able to brush my teeth, being able to shave. But one inconvenience reigned over all the others—no baths.

After fifteen days on the mountain without so much as a "spit bath," I wanted a hot shower! The only cleaning I'd had was done by rubbing snowballs on myself. Once we had our gear consolidated into one big package, ready for the taxi service that would take us to Anchorage the next day, we hit the showers.

We stank! It was understandable, but that didn't make it any more pleasant.

At all times on the mountain, it was important to keep warm. That meant we had to keep on our clothing, regardless of the sweat and natural body dirt. And of course, there's no way to wash clothes while on the mountain. Once in a while, we might

161

peel off our thermals if it was too warm, then put them back on when the temperatures dropped. Every time we had crawled into our sleeping bags, the pungent aroma of body odor reminded us that we needed baths.

Now sleeping bags, hiking clothes, thermals—everything—were stuffed in bags until we could clean them back in Spokane.

Finally, in the blessed hot shower at the bunkhouse, I closed my eyes and let the water pulsate against my face and chest. It took several minutes of scrubbing to eradicate the layers of grime and sweat from my skin. Next came the hair. Three shampoos later, my hair squeaked clean between my fingers. As I shaved the two weeks' growth of beard from my face, I felt like one of the Bible prophets coming off a religious fast.

I examined the finished product in the mirror—and laughed out loud. With the beard gone, I looked like a raccoon! I was tan around the eyes and white where the beard had been. I decided to keep the longer length of hair as part of my mountain man image. With a pair of clean blue jeans and a Summit America sweat shirt, I was ready to face the world.

Well, almost.

I could barely walk. The ball of my foot hurt terribly. The rest of it was numb. The nails of my big toe and the toe next to it were blistered and blackened.

I pulled on a pair of heavy socks. I couldn't tolerate the thought of shoes. I limped over to the telephone and called my parents to tell them the good news. Then I called Fred. His love and commitment to me as his friend had been such an encouragement all along the way.

It was Fred who encouraged me first. "Whatever you need, I will support you on this thing," he'd said at the very beginning.

When I heard his voice, I almost choked.

"We did it, Fred. We did it."

Immediately he came back with, "I never doubted that you would."

We talked for some time about the climb and about my push to the standing high point time from McKinley. I promised to keep him informed of our progress on the rest of the climbs.

When I hung up, I headed to the general store to get something to eat. My problem was making a decision. After eating rehydrated food for two weeks, everything looked good.

That same day we attended the funeral for the two Koreans who had died on the mountain. Parents, wives, children, and friends of the two men, supported by a number of climbers, huddled together as the pastor from the Korean Presbyterian church in Anchorage spoke a few words over the open caskets.

One of the rangers broke down as he read a poem for his friend, the Korean instructor who had died in the accident. I gazed at the grieving faces, and I thought about the two men—young, vigorous, healthy—whose lives ended so abruptly. Besides being more experienced at mountain climbing, they weren't much different from myself. Once again, I thanked God for my safe return.

When the mourners left, I wandered through the little graveyard, reading the names of famous climbers who had died on the mountain. In many cases, their bodies still rested on the mountain in some bottomless crevasse or isolated glacier.

By good fortune, the Polish climber who Jim, the ranger at the 14,000-foot camp, told me about was in town. We arranged to have lunch together. Over a bowl of vegetable soup, Christoff's round, red face became animated as he told me about his ordeal on the Great One.

"Three days the storm battered me. I thought I'd die. As it is . . ." he glanced down at his legs, then back at me, "as it is, I lost both legs below the knees." He spoke so matter-of-factly that I couldn't help but admire his spirit.

We quickly became friends. I told him about my life and my goal to break the high point record. We talked about the emotional impact our amputations had on each of us and how we coped with the loss.

"So, Christoff, where do you go from here?"

"If all goes well, I plan to climb 'er again next year." His face beamed with eager anticipation.

"Hey, that's great, man." And looking at him, I truly believed he would do it.

During the meal, a reporter came to interview me about

the climb. I glanced at Christoff during the interview and saw a trace of sadness that it wasn't he who was being interviewed for doing the climb.

We arranged to meet again in Anchorage for a genuine Polish meal at his home. The next day we drove to Anchorage, where we said goodbye to Adrian, then shared a Polish meal of stuffed cabbage and potatoes with Christoff and his friends. Later we enjoyed a delicious Japanese meal at Mike's friends' home. We were making up for all those rehydrated meals we ate on the mountain.

When we finally arrived back in Spokane and unloaded our gear, it quickly became obvious that our first order of business was to wash our soiled clothing. In some cases, it took as many as three washings to get the body odors out of our polypropylene underwear, pants, and shirts.

When I sniffed the garments, I wasn't sure if they still stank or if the odor was embedded in my mind.

Still hobbling due to my injured toes, I marveled every time I walked across the kitchen floor that I was in a real house, walking on a firm foundation.

During the next two days, I wrestled with the thought of stopping. There were several mountains to go, difficult ones, and I wasn't sure I wanted to do it. And I was no longer certain that the record could be broken.

You don't have to go on, I told myself. *You can quit right now. Why put yourself at such a risk again? McKinley is a big-enough accomplishment. Can't you be satisfied with that?*

Alone in my room, I would pray, "What do You want me to do, God? I know You love me. I know You will protect me, but tell me, should I quit now?"

As proud as I was to have scaled McKinley, I still wanted to break the record. I had been telling everyone our goal was to set a new record and prove that any obstacles could be overcome.

The master plan for Summit America was for the climbs to take place in three stages—the easier peaks first, then McKinley, then the last few difficult western mountains.

The next obstacle was Washington's high point—Mt. Rainier.

When I called Lisa that night, she asked for my projected climbing schedule so she could coordinate the media coverage. "A representative from Hooked on Phonics wants to be at the Mauna Kea climb in Hawaii."

The mere mention of Mauna Kea, the last high point to climb, produced butterflies in my stomach. I had dreamed of the day for so long. *Once we summit Rainier, we're home free!*

In Spokane, we stopped at an REI store and spent another $1,200.00 on gear, including plastic boots necessary for snow and ice climbing. On our way from Spokane to the base camp the next morning, we came around a corner, and there it was—the awe-inspiring Mount Rainier.

Shafts of light illuminated the snow to a vibrant white, contrasting with the intense blue of the sky and the green of the giant firs. Fourteen thousand, four hundred and ten feet high, the mountain's exquisite beauty took my breath away. Again the words of the psalmist came to my lips. "I will fit up mine eyes unto the hills from whence cometh my help. My help cometh from the Lord who made heaven and earth."

I had once heard that by *help*, the author meant strength, a spiritual vitality that comes from faith in God and in one's purpose for living. *How appropriate*, I thought. *I need all the strength I can get to challenge this incredible mountain.*

Mount Rainier, or Mount Tacoma, as it is called by the local Native Americans, is classified as a dormant volcano. Dormant, not extinct. Storms sweeping off the Pacific Ocean as well as squalls produced on the mountain itself make climbing hazardous at any time of the year. Dr. George Draper, a famous psychologist, once said, "Man is at his worst when pitted against his fellow man. He is at his best when pitted against nature." By looking at the mountain's rugged majesty, I knew Mount Rainier would demand my best.

Once we reached the lodge at the trail head, I asked everyone I met if they could recommend a team we could join or a solo climber who could join us. Lisa had arranged for media coverage, so while looking for a climber, I did a couple of newspaper interviews at the park service hotel and met with the rangers. Not finding anyone who could climb with us, my stress increased.

We spent the night at Lee Whitaker's Bunkhouse and Coffee Shop. (Lee Whitaker was a legend in the world of rock climbing, and his brother was the first American to summit Everest.)

As I climbed out of the truck to check in the following morning, I prayed, "Please, Lord, send us another climber. I want this climb to be safe." Neither Whit nor I had enough experience in crevasse rescue, even after McKinley.

We began our ascent up Mt. Rainier from Paradise Inn. We met numerous other climbers hiking along the Skyline Trail. Many of them were day climbers, not intending to go past the Muir Snowfields.

Several hours later, we reached Muir Camp at 10,000 feet. Whit tossed his gear onto an open bunk. Choosing a bunk nearby, I rolled out my sleeping bag and took out my tape recorder to record the day's events. I had barely stretched out on the bag when a stranger burst through the door of the bunkhouse. "I understand there are two guys who are looking for a climbing partner."

I snapped alert. "That's us. My name's Todd Huston." I extended my hand.

"Hi, I'm Jim. Do you mind if I rope up with you?"

"Absolutely not." Then, on second thought, I became cautious. "Have you done much climbing?"

The guy chuckled. "Some. I climbed in the Himalayas and the Alps."

"That's good enough for me." I grinned and shook his hand again. "Welcome to the team."

We left the lodge around midnight, behind another climbing team. By letting them go ahead, they would cut the trail through the new snow, saving us time and concern that we might be on the wrong trail. The moon was full, so we could climb without headlamps.

After crossing the Cowlite Glacier and the loose rock of the Cathedral Rocks, we walked up Ingraham Glacier, a field of snow and ice edged on both sides by major crevasses. At the base of a massive ice wall, we stopped to rest.

"This is the place," the climber warned us, "where a chunk of glacier broke apart and fell down the slope, killing a number of high-school climbers." I looked up at the wall of broken ice. It seemed ready to tumble down on us at any minute.

We traversed across the glacier to the base of Disappointment Cleaver. Next was steep trail with loose gravel. With our ice axes and crampons, we scraped along in the dark trying to follow a makeshift path through the cracks in the rocks.

A long, steep path led to the crater at the top. Finally, we crossed the snow-filled crater to the true summit—Columbia Point.

A sixty-mile-an-hour wind whipped around us, forcing us to put on an extra windbreaker to stay warm. We located the outcropping of the three rocks that signifies the official summit and registered our climb.

After snapping the usual pictures, I located Mt. Adams to the south of us; what was left of Mt. St. Helens; and Oregon's Mt. Hood, our next destination.

On the way down the mountain, I met climbers who had heard about me on the radio, in the newspapers, or on television. Lisa's hard work was paying off. We came to a snow bridge and decided, to be safe, we would belay across. We tested each step with our ice axes, searching for soft spots that might be hiding crevasses. I peered down a number of the blue-green crevasses, trying to see the bottom.

When we reached a smooth, gradual slope, I dropped to my bottom. "Let's glissade!" Like a kid on a toboggan, I glided down the snowfield.

Toward the end of the descent, I met an adolescent who seemed to lack the motivation to learn. He didn't want to work for good grades or participate in school activities. As we walked, I told him about the adventure of climbing and what it had come to mean to me. I shared with him my faith in God and how God had made my success possible. "I know you can't see it now, but school is important. If you ever want to land a high-paying job or make something of yourself, you need to get a good education."

Following me into the lodge, he asked a lot of questions about my life and why I did what I did. It felt good to know that I had reached him—at least in some small way.

I went in search of a pay phone to call Lisa. In the pit of my stomach, I had an eerie feeling that Mt. Hood was going to be more of an adventure than I had previously imagined.

Despite my uncertainty, I told Lisa, "The rest is going to be a breeze. Rainier was the last big hurdle. How are you doing at finding a guide for Hood?"

"No luck so far. I've called every guide service in the Portland Yellow Pages, and no one is going up the mountain this week."

I rubbed my eyes with my hand. "We're so close to breaking the record. Hood is number forty-seven. There must be someone." I knew climbing Hood without a third party would be foolish. Like on Rainier, Whit and I lacked adequate experience on rescue techniques.

I called the headquarters of a recommended guide company and talked with the owner. I told him about our goal to break the current high point record, then reviewed with him the route we wished to follow. His answer left my heart in my socks.

"If you climb that mountain, buddy, it's a death ride."

CHAPTER TWENTY-ONE

Held Hostage by Mt. Hood

Unlike McKinley, the danger on Mt. Hood was not the cold, but the heat. An unexpected heat wave had melted the snow at the summit, exposing dirt and rock. During the colder part of the day, the ice could hold the rocks to the mountains, but when the unseasonably warmer temperatures increased, the ice melted and the rocks cut loose, tumbling down the mountain.

I called Lisa back and reported my failure. "They say it's too dangerous."

"I'll keep trying," she assured me. "I'm sure that once I get to Portland, we'll be able to find an experienced guide somewhere who's willing to climb the mountain."

Lisa would be staying with her brother while we climbed Mt. Hood. This would be the last time we would see each other before flying to Hawaii.

"Hey . . ." I felt a tap on my shoulder. It was Whit. "Ready to roll?"

I nodded, wished Lisa a safe flight, and followed Whit out to the truck.

"Find a guide?"

I climbed into the passenger seat. "Not yet." My foot ached, my stump ached; my back ached; my head ached. The last thing I felt like doing was driving the three hours south to

Portland to face another problem.

Whit glanced over at me as he eased the truck onto the highway. "What will we do if you can't find a guide?"

I leaned my head against the backrest and closed my eyes. "I don't know." We had both heard of the accident on Mt. Hood a week earlier. A team of five climbers fell. Two were killed, and two others were severely injured. "Every one of the guide services recommends we stay off the mountain."

"That's easy for them to say," Whit mumbled. "They don't have a record to break!"

Weary beyond words, I sighed. "I understand where they're coming from. They have their liability insurance to consider as well as their reputations for safety."

Exhaustion from the climb and from the stress of our situation lulled me into a semiconscious rest. When we hit the outskirts of Portland, we headed straight for a hotel.

Whit staggered down the hallway ahead of me. Upon reaching his door, he waved his hand in the air. "See ya next week."

Once inside my room, I puttered about, taking a shower and placing a call home to my folks. I thought about Lisa flying into Portland International Airport and her brother being there to meet her. And the more I thought about her, the more I knew I should go meet her at the airport. *I should go meet her flight. I appreciate having her meet me when I fly home. And it would be a kick to surprise her.*

I flopped onto the bed, stared up at the ceiling, and yawned. "I'm too tired." I closed my eyes. Suddenly they flew open. I sat up and ran my fingers through my disheveled hair. "This is not going to work. I might as well face it. I want to go to the airport more than I want to sleep."

I hauled on my T-shirt, shorts, and shoe, strapped on my artificial leg, ran a comb through my hair, and headed out the door.

Her brother recognized me from the news clipping she had mailed him. While we waited for the plane to arrive, we talked. I eagerly moved closer to the cordoned area and watched until she exited the jetway.

"Todd! I didn't expect to see you here!" she squealed, throwing her arms about my neck." I gave her a long hug. So much had happened since the last time I had seen her. We discussed our guide problem all the way to the car. She had good news.

"I found a guide service that will take you up the mountain."

Suddenly I felt much better.

The next day she and Whit went sightseeing in Portland while I talked with the guide service. Eight hours before we were scheduled to do the climb, I got a message from them.

"No," I shouted. "You can't back out now!" But they did. I had little choice but to resume my search.

I called another guide service. "No way, man." They wouldn't even listen to my plans. Next I called a man Whit had met on Rainier who had agreed to climb with us.

"Sorry. I can't do it."

"But you said . . ."

"That was before I heard the updates on the condition of the mountain. There are rocks the size of refrigerators tumbling down the slopes!"

I closed my eyes and rubbed the back of my neck. I had heard it all before.

"The snow bridge is gone," he continued. "We would have less than a fifty-fifty chance of coming out alive."

My head pounded from the tension knots in my neck. "What if we do an alternate route?"

"You'd be in even bigger trouble. Why don't you come back in a week or so?"

"I can't do that," I told him. "Besides, it's only July. The longer we wait, the more the snow will melt and the worse the mountain will get."

I hung up the receiver. *Maybe they're all right. Maybe I would be a fool to go up there now. Maybe I should call off the rest of the expedition.* Discouraged, I called Fred in Reno. *If anyone can tell me what to do, he can,* I thought.

Fred had climbed Mt. Elbrus in Russia, Killamanjaro in Africa, and Aconcanqua in South America. The phone rang three times before I heard Kathy's voice. "Fred and I cannot come to the phone right now, but if at the beep, you'll leave your message . . ."

"Auggh!!" I groaned. "Where are you, dude?" I left a message, pouring out my sad plight.

The next day Fred called. "Todd, I think the mountain can be climbed. You've come too far to quit now. If you'll send me the plane fare, I'll get you up Mt. Hood."

The next morning at 9:30 I met Fred at the airport. He threw his bag into the truck. "Let's go climb a mountain," he said.

I drove him to the hotel, where we talked with Whit and Lisa about the climb.

"What if it's dangerous?" Lisa asked.

Fred shrugged. "If there's a problem, we'll find a way around it. We won't climb if it's not safe. I promise."

"Good." I sighed with relief. "No mountain is worth dying over. I'm willing to take reasonable risks, but I don't want to make stupid mistakes."

I thought of the possibility of failure. *I can tell people we really tried. We gave it our best shot.* Yet, in my heart I knew that the impact would be nowhere near as great as breaking the record would be. *OK, Lord, here goes. As usual, it's in Your hands.*

We all piled into the truck and headed east, across the Morrison Bridge. Mt. Hood floated above the city like a fantasy mountain, unattainable and aloof.

We ate at Timberline Lodge and talked to the park rangers about the hazards.

The soft crunch of snow under my plastic boot settled into a comfortable rhythm as I followed Fred up the base of the mountain. The early evening's warmer temperatures allowed us to do the lower part of the mountain while wearing hiking shorts and long-sleeved shirts. Later on, we would add the layers of heavy clothing the higher altitudes would demand.

We continued hiking to where the pathway turned into a trail. Lisa ran ahead of us, then dropped behind us, snapping photos of Whit, Fred, and me as we climbed. When the trail grew rougher, we bade her goodbye, and she returned to the lodge while Whit, Fred, and I continued up the mountain.

"Come on." Fred waved his arm. "Let's do it!"

I gingerly tested my weight in the snow beside the trail. "The snow is good and solid."

Whit kicked at a clump of snow with the toe of his hiking boot. "Feels OK."

Satisfied, Fred turned and headed up the ski slope.

Trudging up the hill beyond the ski area, my boot and the foot of my artificial limb kept sinking into the soft ground and sliding back a half step for every step I took forward. Fred adjusted his pace accordingly. A mile or so above the second lodge, we paused to watch the sunset toward the west. The air temperatures dropped quickly, forcing us into our heavier clothing.

From our position on the mountain, we could see the city of Portland as the colors faded against the hills to the west of the city. One after another, we watched the lights blink on until they were like diamond chips scattered across a stretch of dark blue velvet.

Fred suggested, "If we get up there fast enough, I'll climb ahead of you and set up camp, then scout the mountain to find out what's happening." He repeated our game plan. "We'll camp at Hog'sback Ridge, directly below the summit. We'll sleep from midnight to 4:00 a.m., the absolute coldest hour of the night, then charge to the summit and rush back down away from the rocks as quickly as possible."

The crisp night air stung my cheeks and invigorated my step as we hiked across rock-strewn ridges. Using our ice axes but not our crampons, we crossed a field of snow and ice. *If you slip here, Todd,* I told myself, *you're going to take one long sleigh ride.*

We came to the base of a treacherous slope of solid ice, the last measure of ice before cresting at Hogsback Ridge. The only light was from our headlamps. Fred pointed toward the top. "There it is. Let's go on up."

I had barely made it the top of the ridge we were standing on. Looking up at the slick surface on the walls of the ridge, then down from whence I had already climbed, I pulled my crampons out of my pack. "Looks a little icy. I'm going to put these on first."

"Aw, it's not that bad," Fred scoffed, "but you go ahead and put 'em on. I'm heading on up."

He did too. All of five feet. Then, struggling to catch his

footing, he spun out, like a lightweight car accelerating on an icy hill. When he regained his footing, he inched back down the wall in a controlled slide. He slid to a stop and grinned. "I think I'll put my crampons on now." Whit and I laughed.

Step by step, we inched up the slope to the top of a 200-foot ridge. All conversation and banter ceased. To take each step required total concentration. One wrong step, and a person could roll down to the gnarled outcroppings spewed from the mountain during a more violent chapter in its life. Massive, piano-sized rocks that had tumbled from the cliff and rolled a thousand yards or more dotted the ice field below.

Near the upper reaches of Klickatat Glacier, we could see sulfur fumes belching from the crevasses, like steam from a giant railroad engine buried deep within the mountain. Legend says that Native American tribes never climbed beyond Mt. Hood's glaciers, for they believed that the crest of the mountain was the kingdom of the spirits, a place taboo to humans.

If we started sliding at this point on the mountain, we could roll into puddles of water—snow melted by the heat coming from deep inside the mountain. We hacked our way to the top of the ridge. Steep slopes fell away from each side of the foot-and-a-half-wide ridge. We hiked along the top until we found a wider spot (a couple of feet wider) and made camp.

Removing our packs, we anchored them to the mountain. With our ice axes, we each carved out individual campsites large enough to spread out one sleeping bag. Next, we piled snow along the downhill edge of our bags. Hopefully, that would prevent us from rolling down the side of the mountain in our sleep.

Once satisfied with our fortresses, we pounded our axes into the snow and tied our sleeping bags to them. With any luck, my ax would keep my sleeping bag from sliding down the 200- to 300-foot slope into a deep gully where the ice had melted away from the rock.

If a person slid, his body might never be recovered.

CHAPTER TWENTY-TWO

Mt. Whitney—Number Forty-nine

"Phew!" Whit straightened up and wrinkled his nose. "What stinks?"

Fred laughed. "The sulfur fumes."

We ate handfuls of gorp, or trail mix, drank hot cider, then fell asleep watching the tendrils of smoke coming out of the side of the mountain. At 4:00 a.m., I shivered in the sub-Arctic temperatures as we packed the barest of our essentials into our summit packs. A cold front had moved in while we slept, bringing even lower temperatures than we had hoped for, thank God.

I put on my helmet, strapped myself into my climbing harness, roped up, and started up the ridge. I glanced down the ridge where we had climbed earlier and spotted other climbers behind us. They spotted us as well and stopped so that they wouldn't be at risk from any rocks we might accidentally send rolling down the slope.

We came to a burgstrom, a crevasse or series of crevasses at the upper end of a glacier where the glacier is breaking away from the mountain. The sight stopped us in our tracks.

A narrow tongue of snow stretched across a chasm. This was the snow bridge the guides and the rangers had said no longer existed. Whit and I braced ourselves as Fred tested the bridge to see how strong it was. "It's OK," he called back as he shifted his feet across the open crevasse. Once he reached the other side and secured his ice ax into the mountain, he signaled for me to cross.

I held my breath and inched across the bridge of snow and ice, certain that at any moment I would break through and find myself swinging like a spider on a thread, a thousand or more feet above eternity. I resumed normal breathing on the other side. Whit came safely across behind me.

Our next challenge was the sight of a killer rock fall. Normally, snow covered these rocks, but due to the warming temperatures, we climbed up a sluice of loose rock, dirt, and ice. My crampons refused to dig into the mottled surface. Every step dislodged more rocks, sending them tumbling down the mountain. Fred went ahead and stopped to wait for me to cross. Then Whit followed me.

The slope grew steeper until we were crawling over the larger rocks. Suddenly, my foot broke a rock loose from the mountain, sending it crashing to the valley below. I dug my crampon into a crag in a nearby rock. "Oh, dear God, give me good footholds," I prayed.

We passed the crux of the mountain, crawling up a gully of snow, ice, loose rock, and mud. With my hands and my clothing coated with mud, I scrambled to the ridge in time to see the sun rise over the mountain ranges to the east.

"There it is, boys." Fred rushed ahead, turned, and shouted, "We're here!"

Whit and I rushed to the top, high-fived one another, and signed the register.

"Pictures! Time for pictures." Fred set his camera on a rock, set the automatic timer, then ran to where Whit and I waited. The camera clicked. "One more," he shouted. We repeated the process with each other's cameras.

Even though we needed to hurry off the summit, I paused. My gaze swept the horizon. I was standing on the back of a gargantuan, restless, smoke-belching monster. To the east, I could see a succession of mountain ranges flattening out into a high chaparral; to the south, Mt. Jefferson, named by Lewis and Clark after the president who funded their exploration, and the Three Sisters, sentinels west of Bend. I turned to-

Whit and I at the summit of Maine's high point, Mt. Katadin. With the beautiful scenery came black flies, mosquitoes, heat and humidity. It was one of our most miserable climbs.

Always a welcome sight! These USGS metal markers would often be placed on the high points. I personally jumped on every one I saw!

A typical eastern high point—a rock surrounded by trees.

A grouchy neighbor tried to block the path to Rhode Island's high point with his van. We snuck past before he saw us.

Whit and I celebrate reaching the high point of Massachusetts, Mt. Greylock. A war memorial sits at the top of the mountain.

A most dangerous high point! Delaware's Ebright Azimuth sits right in the middle of a street. We had to try three times to get this shot without getting run over!

This is why they call them the "Smoky" Mountains. A beautiful, if foggy, panorama in Tennessee.

A foggy day at the summit of North Carolina's high point.

On my way up Mt. Rogers, Virginia

Many high points, like this one in Georgia, are marked by historical sign points.

The lowest high point in the country—in Florida.

Without Lisa's faith and hard-working support, the Summit America expedition would never have made it.

Eagle Mountain, the high point of Minnesota.

Our hike up Eagle Mountain led us across these wooden walkways over the Boundary Waters Canoe Area—mosquito heaven!

At the highest point in Kansas, we found Mt. Sunflower. The sunflower is constructed out of welded railroad spikes.

I met this group of lively students on Oklahoma's high point, Black Mesa. This large mesa has steep cliff sides. On the way down, this teacher slipped and broke her ankle. I led the kids the rest of the way while Whit helped carry the teacher down.

Even on the highest mountain in Texas, Guadalupe Peak, it was hot. We climbed at night, because it was 118 degrees that day!

Camping on Froze-to-Death Plateau on the way to Granite Peak in Montana. The rangers warn climbers to watch out for blizzards on Froze-to-Death even in the summer. The rock-wall shelters help protect climbers from wind and snow.

From Tempest Peak, we could see our destination—Granite Peak. We climbed from the slope on the left.

Me, Whit and Mike at the summit of Granite Peak.

I made it to the top! Nevada's Boundary Peak sits right on the border of Nevada and California. The Sierra-Nevada Mountains in the distance made a beautiful sight.

One of the more dangerous climbs, Borah Peak in Idaho, had a knife's edge ridge with a dizzying dropoff on both sides.

Barbara and I (and Kona) resting at Island Lake during the climb of Gannett Peak in Wyoming.

On a nice summer day, Mike and Barbara and I near the summit of Gannett Peak.

Gannett Peak and the Wind River Range had the most beautiful scenery of any climb.

The McKinley team—Whit, Mike, Adrian, and me. The beautiful red chariot would carry us up to the glacier.

My last meal? I'm not sure I even tasted the pizza, but Mike and Adrian were more relaxed.

We flew through One-Shot Pass on our way to Kahiltna Glacier.

Although this Korean climber didn't speak English, he was inspired by my attempt to climb. Many other climbers lent their support and encouragment along the way.

Without being roped up, it would be foolish to stand next to this beautiful, but deadly, crevasse.

We headed up Kahiltna Glacier, a vast expanse of ice and snow, loaded up with gear and pulling sleds. As strange as it sounds, we worked to avoid sunburn and frostbite at the same time.

Here at Denali Pass, a recent accident claimed the life of another climber. Mike rests on his ice axe while making the summit approach from the 17,000-foot camp.

A typical group campsite or tent city, crowded with climbers. The snow walls offered protection from the weather.

Resting between climbs to get acclimated, I took a few minutes to read a book.

Not your usual ranger station! This tent at the 14,000-foot camp served as the ranger station and offered assistance and information for climbers.

Roped together, the team climbs the West Buttress.

We dug out a campsite and space for a kitchen. No one left the immediate campsite without being roped up.

Thank you, God! I'm standing at the summit of Denali, the top of North America!

The team poses for a sponsor shot with the "Hooked on Phonics" T-shirts. No one offered to change into one . . .

Whit, Fred the "copycat," and I at the Timberline Lodge before we start up Mt. Hood.

Using ski poles helped me on the climb up the awesomely beautiful Mt. Rainier.

Fred, Lisa, Whit and I stop by to encourage a young handicapped girl and her family on our way to Mt. Hood.

When I stood at this point, I knew we had done it. Mt. Whitney was the forty-ninth and last real climb—only Mauna Kea remained. We rolled out our sleeping bags and slept "higher" than anyone else in the lower forty-eight states.

There were many congratulatory banners as we arrived a Mauna Kea. Hawaii's volcanic high point is in the background.

More personal congratulations from a beautiful Hawaiian at the luau.

The final climb leads up Mauna Kea's moon-like surface.

The Flex-foot VSP with Vivram boot-sole glued to the bottom. This leg carried me every step of the way!

I was impressed over and over with the beauty of the mountains—and the people I met (Mt. Wheeler, New Mexico).

My now tradional victory pose on top of Mt. Whitney at sunset. It's amazing what God can do with us if we have faith in Him and the abilities He's given us.

ward the north and followed, with my eyes, the Columbia Gorge and the famous river that challenged the pioneers. Facing west, I could see the lights in the city of Portland blinking off for another day.

"Todd." I felt Fred's hand on my shoulder. "I'm glad you asked me to do this climb with you."

I smiled. "Me too. You don't know how important you've been to the entire expedition. Getting us up a mountain no one else was willing to . . ."

"Yes," he interrupted, "but you're the one who's gone the distance. This climb is yours, remember?"

Silently we stood side by side for several minutes watching the morning come to the valleys below—two lifelong friends sharing our moment of triumph.

Fred picked up his pack. "Hey, dude, we gotta get on out of here."

Reluctantly I tightened the strap on my helmet and prepared to leave. It was the same feeling on every difficult summit—so much work and so little time to enjoy the accomplishment.

I would have loved to stay on the mountain longer, to study the ever-changing moods of the terrain. I wondered what it would be like to lie under the canopy of stars or watch the moon rise from the perspective of the summit. The mountain seemed permanent, unshakable. Again, I felt the presence of an unseen Power.

Once we started down, I remembered my concern about the climb down. The route would be more dangerous since the sun was up. We watched each other carefully as we started down the trail, leaving only our faint footprints behind and our signatures in the register to prove we had been there.

We roped up and took a different chute down the mountain. While it was very slippery, the descent itself was much easier. When we reached the rocks, I stopped to take off my crampons. Whit stayed with me while Fred ran ahead to begin packing away the gear. He had a plane to catch in Portland.

"Todd, can you be down by nine?" Fred asked.

"I'll give it my best shot."

Fred waved and ran full-pack down the mountain. A few minutes later, Whit and I got back on the trail. When we reached the ski slope area, I laid down on my back and glissaded down the mountain while Whit ran.

Finding a safe area, I glissaded past skiers and snow boarders. After passing the smaller lodge, I glissaded a bit, then took off running. I had seen Fred do it, and I wanted to try it for myself.

Throwing my head back to the wind, I picked up speed. Suddenly, without any warning, my artificial leg blew out beneath me, sending me sprawling into the snow.

Somehow, it didn't even hurt. In fact, I liked it! The clip that held the spring in my leg had popped off, so I pawed through my pack until I found a spare, then started running down the trail again. I made it to Timberline Lodge only twenty minutes behind Fred. Whit was right behind.

After stashing our gear in the truck, we loaded into the cab and headed for Portland International Airport. After a wild trip, with tires squealing on some of the curves, Whit pulled the truck to a stop in front of the departing gate five minutes before takeoff.

Fred leapt out of the truck and reached for his gear.

"Leave it," I shouted. "We'll bring it to Reno tomorrow."

Fred nodded and dashed into the terminal. Lisa and I followed behind, in case he missed his flight. At the gate, I asked the attendant if Fred made it.

She nodded. "The door to the jetway was already closed. We had to open it for him."

We dropped Lisa off at her brother's home. She would fly back to California to finalize the Hawaii plans while we headed down I-5 for Nevada. We cheered when we crossed the Oregon-California border, though we were still more than 500 miles from home. We had experienced the same exhilaration when we crossed into the Pacific Time Zone. We had crossed the different time zone lines twenty-seven times during our trip.

We stayed with Fred and Kathy that night and the next day, then drove south out of Reno to Boundary Peak, Nevada's 13,143-foot high point.

Located down a desolate road on the California-Nevada border, the desert peak is considered to be a strenuous climb. To me, the most strenuous part of the climb was having no source of drinking water along the 7.4-mile trail.

Looking west at the horizon, Whit and I tried to guess which mountain peak was Mt. Whitney, our forty-ninth climb. We relaxed on top, enjoying the scenery. While I returned by the same trail we had climbed, Whit chose to walk back by another trail, one he had seen from the summit. As I walked through a wide valley, I heard a neigh. I whipped about in time to see a pack of wild horses. Nearby, a young colt stood close to its mother's side. Suddenly the mare saw me and reared up on its hind legs. "Hey, guys." I backed slowly away. "It's OK."

Seeing a bush off to one side, I ducked behind it, then circumvented the area. They, too, moved cautiously in the other direction, both of us hedging one another.

Whit was asleep in the front seat by the time I reached the truck. After I slaked my thirst with what seemed like a gallon of water, I tossed my gear in the back of the truck and climbed aboard, and we headed toward California's John Muir Wilderness and Mt. Whitney.

Whit had arranged to meet David Long, one of his buddies, at a motel in the town of Lone Pine. David wanted to hike the last mountain on the continental United States with us. Because an overnight camping permit is required for Mt. Whitney and the permits are issued at the ranger's station by lottery each morning, we turned in early that evening. The worst thing I could imagine would be to have the rangers run out of permits before we got one.

The next morning while I called Lisa to settle the last-minute details before she flew to Hawaii, Whit drove to the ranger station and acquired the necessary camping permit. By eleven that morning, we were on the trail. We projected an eight-and-a-half-hour trek, four hours to the trail camp, a half-hour to rest, then four hours from there to the summit.

Whit and his friend started out ahead of me from Whitney Portal, where we left the truck. Muscles hardened by a summer of climbing and spirits pumped to complete the last climb before Hawaii, I moved with speed and agility up the trail. Whenever I passed other climbers, I stopped and talked awhile; then I would speed up to resume my climb. I felt like a well-tuned machine as I hiked over streams and past lakes with ease. How different this climb was from my earliest mountain experiences.

At the Outpost Camp, I met a recent high-school graduate and her mother climbing the mountain. After hearing my story, the girl admitted to her fears of beginning college in the fall, her personal challenge to climb. Another young woman whom I chatted with near the Trail Crest talked about her engagement and upcoming marriage. I wished her the best.

I knew the challenge of Mt. Whitney was the switchbacks— ninety-seven of them, winding up the hillside. (Whit counted them.) I had been dreading them from the moment I first heard about them from other climbers. As I maneuvered them, I was surprised that the switchbacks were not the negatives I imagined them to be, but instead, positives that made the climb much easier.

Walls of sheer rock edged the well-marked trail. In the distance, pinnacles, tall sentinels of the trail, rose up around me. I could see how Clarence King, a member of the Whitney survey team, could have made two attempts to be the first to climb the mountain, and both times climbed the wrong peak. Without the well-marked trail, it would be difficult to tell which pinnacle to climb. Mr. King named the mountain after his boss, Josiah D. Whitney, the chief of the State Geological Survey from 1860-1874.

I caught up with Whit and his friend at the Trail Camp. We stopped to pump water from the lake with our purifiers before continuing. Halfway up the 14,494-foot mountain, I couldn't feel the lower oxygen levels. However, I could see signs of fatigue in Whit's friend's movements and face.

Concerned, I handed him half a tablet of the medicine the doctor in Alaska gave me for altitude sickness. "Keep it handy just in case we get separated or something," I advised. "It helps."

We resumed our climb to the summit. The sun was going down as we reached the ridge connecting the pinnacles and gaps with the registered high point. From the ridge, I could see clear to the town of Lone Pine and across the desolate high plains of eastern Nevada.

A helicopter landed on top of the mountain, then took off again. I wondered why. Since climbing McKinley, I associated helicopters with emergencies.

Walking several yards farther, I spotted the small stone hut, built and maintained by the Smithsonian Institute at the summit, for the convenience of Mt. Whitney's hikers.

"Yes!" I broke into a run despite the fact that I had been hiking for eight hours. Adrenaline pumped through my body as I charged up the last few yards to the summit. The altitude didn't slow me down this time. I threw my hands into the air. "Yeah! We made it!"

An orange glow filled the sky, topping off the incredible wave of happiness that washed through me. Another challenge met, another victory gained. Barring an unforeseen accident, I knew we were home free.

After registering and taking the usual photographs, the three of us headed toward the sleeping hut. I asked a young man nearby about the helicopter.

"Some guy got a bad case of elevation sickness and had to be flown to the hospital."

After Whit made dinner, I took my cellular phone out of my backpack and dialed Fred's number in Reno.

"Hi, Kathy. This is Todd. Fred there?"

Several seconds passed before I heard my friend's voice.

"Hi, Fred. I'm calling you from the summit of Mt. Whitney! We made it. Saturday morning we'll fly out of Los Angeles International for Hawaii. Can you believe it?"

Next, I called the talk show host in Hawaii who had been following my climb. "I'll see you Sunday when we break the world's record."

CHAPTER TWENTY-THREE

More Than Mountains

Palm trees waving in the soft Pacific breeze, azure blue surf lapping the pearly white sand, suntanned children splashing in the surf—a far cry this was from the deadly ice crevasses of McKinley, the stinging black flies of Katahdin, and my unslaked thirst on New Mexico's Wheeler Peak! I pulled my Hooked on Phonics T-shirt over my head and strode over to the mirror to comb my recently trimmed hair.

A knock sounded at the door. "Come on, Todd." My little brother Steve, a student at Brown University, had flown to Hawaii with my mother for my last climb. "Lisa told us to get you to the mountain on time."

"I'm coming, I'm coming."

A strange languor filled me as I considered facing my last mountain. For more than a year, I had anticipated the expedition. I had focused every waking moment on my goal of breaking the high point record. For months, I had trained my body and my mind for the rigors of the climb. For weeks, I had lived for each new mountain. And for days, I had thought of nothing but this morning. *And now I'm here and I seem to need a stick of dynamite to go off beneath me to get me going.*

No life-threatening escape, no death-defying rescue, no gripping drama—just a brief drive up the mountain, followed by an even briefer hike to the summit.

If real life mimicked prime-time television, my story would end with Whit lost during a whiteout on Mt. McKinley and me rescuing him seconds before he gasped his last—if life mimicked TV.

Instead, I found myself worrying about which hiking sock to wear for the cameras. I adjusted my cap on my sun-bleached hair and hurried out to my waiting entourage.

Climbing Mauna Kea, Hawaii's 13,796-foot mountain, would have been anticlimatic after McKinley or Rainier, except for the celebration Lisa had planned. She had already left for the Hale Pohaku Visitor's Center to finish the last-minute media coverage for my arrival.

At the car I met Lori, the representative from Hooked on Phonics. She would transport my mother and Whit to the mountain while my brother and I rode in the back of a friend's pickup truck.

We rode down palm tree–lined boulevards, past luxurious hotels and the accompanying tourist shops, through residential areas similar to many near my home in Southern California, and past the security gates of larger, more palatial estates. Next came lava beds, then green fields of sugar cane and pineapple.

My brother and I recalled all the adventures we had shared during our Boy Scout days and laughed. It seemed like such a short time ago. The driver of our truck laid on the horn as we rounded the last corner before the visitor's center. Lori, driving the car behind us, did the same. Banners waved over the steps of the center.

"Congratulations Todd Huston! from Hooked on Phonics!"

"Congratulations Summit America for Breaking the Record!"

"June 1 to August 7!"

The poles of street lights wore brightly painted posters saying, "Great Job, Todd! You did it!"

Television camera technicians and news reporters swarmed as my brother and I climbed out of the truck bed. Cameras flashed as pretty women draped leis about my neck and kissed me on the cheek.

I did a television interview on the steps of the visitor's center. "Having an amputation is just like having a loved one die," I explained. "You go through the same stages of grief . . .

all your hopes and dreams have been shattered. Then you learn to accept it and realize it's just another hurdle in life to overcome.

"I see myself as a representative of the forty-three million Americans who, on any given day, are struggling against a major illness, a disability, or any other health-related challenge." I went on to include challenges that couldn't be X-rayed—challenges like divorce, the death of a loved one, overweight, or overcoming drug or alcohol addictions.

I continued to smile as the journalist turned toward the camera to wrap up the interview. "Thirty-three-year-old Todd Huston, from California, stands atop our own Mauna Kea at the conclusion of a sixty-seven day journey that took him to the top of the highest peak in each of America's fifty states. Only thirty-two people have ever accomplished this feat, but Huston, the thirty-second, did it in less time. And with fewer legs." (He forgot to mention that Whit had also climbed all the peaks with me.)

Someone yelled, "Cut!"

The reporter thanked me for the interview. Then we streamed inside the visitor's center and listened to a presentation about the mountain. The ranger explained that Mauna Kea is the number-one place in the world to do stargazing. "Many countries have placed observatories on top of the mountain. The observatory complex is called the Onizuka Center for International Astronomy after Air Force Lt. Col. Ellison S. Onizuka, who lost his life on the ill-fated *Challenger* flight."

At the end of the lecture, we climbed into the waiting vehicles for the winding drive to the summit. The greenery grew sparse as we wound our way up the mountain road. When the pavement ended, we parked the truck and started climbing the steep gravel road to the whir of video cameras. Whit, Steve, Lori, and the video crew hiked with me. Before long, the video crew, especially, were huffing and puffing from the altitude change.

Upon reaching the parking lot nearest the summit, I found Lisa and my mother waiting by the car. They had driven on ahead.

"Hey, no fair, you two!" I shouted.

Mom laughed. "Only way to go!"

Lisa climbed out of the car. She and my mother joined the procession of hikers climbing the mountain with me. I glanced toward Lisa and noticed tears filling her eyes.

I looked at my watch. It was almost noon! Up ahead I could see the observatory buildings on the summit. The video cameras rolled while I hiked down a short dip, then up the slope to the top.

This is it, I thought as I stepped on the marker that officially ended the Summit America project. *It's over. We did it.*

I grabbed Lisa and gave her a big hug. "This wouldn't have happened," I choked back my tears, "if it weren't for you." I shot a look of gratitude skyward . . . *Nor without You, Father.*

"Pictures!" one of the photographers shouted.

I gestured to Lisa and Whit to join me. As we posed for the cameras, I raised my hands and shouted, "Thank You, God!"

The photographers filmed me while I talked on the telephone with the local radio station DJ. "Why did you brave the snow and ice, the dizzying heights, and the unbelievable fatigue to break this record?" the radio personality asked.

"It's about more than mountains or mountain climbing," I answered. "I did it to inspire and encourage people. Everyone has challenges. Whether your challenge is physical—like cancer or an amputation—or emotional—the loss of loved one through divorce or death—the challenge can be overcome through hard work and trust in God's guidance."

I had given that answer many, many times since the day I first applied to 50 Peaks Project. But I never meant it more than I did that day standing on the summit of Mauna Kea.

"Tell our listeners about your sponsor, Hooked on Phonics." Again, I related the story of Lisa and her T-shirt stand. "That was a miracle, the way everything came together."

"And now, what challenge is next for Todd Huston?"

I grinned. "I want to get the message out that by having faith in God and belief in yourself, you can overcome whatever you face in life. My new motto is, 'Take a step in faith, and you can do anything!' "

The media frenzy continued for several minutes. When it slacked off, I paused to enjoy the view of Mauna Kea and the tops of clouds spread out below me. *How will I go back to a normal nine-to-five existence after seeing life from this perspective?*

I recalled snippets of the ranger's lecture back at the visitor's center in which he quoted Reverend Martin Luther King's famous "mountaintop" speech. "I've been to the mountaintop, and I've seen the other side." The other side of Mauna Kea is so barren that United States astronauts practiced driving their moon buggies on its pockmarked terrain.

Finally, it was time to leave, to come down off the mountain. I couldn't hold onto the moment any longer. I had climbed my mountains and seen the other side. And now, I wasn't the naive and untested man who had set out across the continent a few months ago in a red Ford pickup truck. I had dodged thunderstorms, battled blizzards, endured incredible pain, and faced my fears through faith in God. I was stronger and, I hope, wiser.

I had a new appreciation for the vastness of my country and its varied loveliness. But more importantly, I had discovered the beauty in the people. Ranger Annie on McKinley; Barbara and her black Lab, Kona; the Sterlers of Iowa; the burned-out chemical engineer; the young woman yearning to escape the confines of the little-town life; the family I met on Cheaha Mountain—honest, friendly, amazing people, each scaling their own personal mountains and barriers.

Most of all, I had gained a deeper experience with God. Time after time, when it seemed like the expedition was doomed, He smoothed the way. Time after time, when my body hurt so badly I thought I couldn't take another step, He infused me with the strength to continue. Time after time, He was there.

Now I know He always will be.

Epilogue

I wanted to repeat my message one more time: By having faith in God and believing in the abilities He's given us, we can overcome whatever challenges we face in life.

We all have challenges. Some are physical, like a leg amputation, heart problems, or hip replacement. Others cannot be seen by X-ray. The death of a loved one, a divorce or separation, or combating an addiction to alcohol or drugs can throw up barriers that seem unconquerable. But they are not.

The pain is often difficult, but perserverance can make the difference between success and failure. If we're willing to hang on through the seemingly unending pain, we'll find that it is only a brief chapter. The lessons learned and the joy that grows from surviving will last an eternity.

So whatever you are facing, be strong and courageous. You are not alone. God and His human helpers are there for you. Faith is that which is hoped for but not yet seen. Have faith that God is there to help you overcome whatever you face.

See you at the top!

Todd Huston

Todd is planning to continue his adventure by climbing the highest elevations of each country in the world. Sharing the message of promise and hope he demonstrated on the Summit America Expedition, he is currently crisscrossing the globe, this time by air.

As part of this new ministry, he is working to bring prosthetics to third-world countries and remote areas of the world.

At schools, he encourages students not to drop out, to overcome the challenges of getting an education.

When speaking at libraries and civic organizations, he emphasizes the importance of integrity and citizenship.

In hospitals, he visits patients and health-care professionals, reminding them that they must work together as a team.

Businesspeople are encouraged to set goals and strive creatively to meet them, while meeting the needs of their customers, their employees, and their community.

Todd Huston is available
for appearances, book signings,
and motivational talks.
To make arrangements, contact:
Huston Resources
P.O. Box 702374
Tulsa, OK 74170
(918) 494-6678